TEAM ME

Using Archetypes to

Get Out of Stuck

by Pad

Copyright

Author: Pad

Title: Team Me ~ Using Archetypes to Get Out of Stuck

Edition 3

© 2012-2015, Pad

Published by: Come Alive Success Coaching ltd.

ISBN-13: 978-1508489795

Table of Contents

"Ask not if you will change the world;

Ask how many worlds you will change."

What People are Saying

"This is a wonderful book that shows you how to unlock your full potential for success and achievement."
Brian Tracy. Multiple Bestselling Business Author

"I had the privilege to work with Pad at the London ICF conference. His work is brilliant!" Team Me is both simple and profound. Get the book... and attend a workshop - how you approach your daily challenges in life will forever be better."
Marcia Reynolds, PsyD. Author of **'Wander Woman'** and **Past President of the International Coach Federation**

"Utterly amazing... As a successful, professional actor I fully understand the power of archetypes. What Pad has achieved in this book is to make their powers and potentials accessible to anyone who is hungry for more in life. The material will provide you not only with a better understanding of yourself but specific methods you can use to step up and deal with things like never before. Brilliant!"
Andy Pandini. Actor & Comedian. Los Angeles

"These [live] sessions have been the most powerful few hours I've experienced in... well, years!"
H. Sohal. Corporate Manager. London

"Pad is the leading authority in archetypes. His amazing work will show you how to access the different archetypes within yourself to improve your results in life."

Matt Kendall. Founder & Host of *Interesting Talks*. London

"His knowledge of how people work, coupled with his fantastic communication skills, makes him a brilliant motivator."

R. Lockie. Creative Director. London

"Pad is an inspiring mentor and trainer with extraordinary communication and people skills. He knows exactly how to challenge people and how to help in developing further."

Matthias Link. Business Owner. Munich

"I just had to tell, you are changing my life! I feel empowered and loving, less afraid, less affected by disapproval. More trusting that everything is working out for the best. The knock on effect in my personal life has been awesome... Thank you so much."

Lisa Magdalena. Relationship Coach. London

Introduction

Is there any part of your life where you simply feel stuck? It's as if you're facing a wall, a roadblock, an impasse of some kind that restricts your progress, steals your joy, limits your potential and confines you to a cage of a *life so ordinary*.

Many people have learned to live with a sense that 'this is our lot' and believe they shouldn't really expect much more from life. Others may have been a little more determined about what they really wanted and have progressed towards their goals: getting a promotion, building strong relationships, achieving financial stability, delivering on a significant project or even making some kind of breakthrough discovery, but they too will probably admit that there are other areas of their lives where they've not done quite so well.

If you feel you fit any of these categories, this book will provide you with an approach that has revolutionised many lives already; helping people break through their ceilings of fear and tap into strengths that have previously lain dormant.

The Story of my Life

By the time I had left school, I had learned that there were many things I really wasn't very good at.

I could name a small handful of things that I could do quite well, things I really enjoyed and spent time on, but it was hard to see how I could make a good living – in fact any kind of living at all – out of any of these things. I would get inspired, I'd progress to a certain level and then, for reasons I could not fully explain, seemed to hit a ceiling, a wall, an impasse. Things would just seem to stall. I would find myself losing interest and soon enough I'd simply give up.

It was many years before I realised that one of the primary reasons for my numerous failed ventures was the way that I'd respond to criticism. I would take just a little criticism from someone - from almost anyone - as a very good reason to give up completely.

Instead of continuing my advance into new and exciting territories, I would retreat into my own world, isolate myself from the people around me (whom I deeply needed and later discovered actually needed me) and disengage from many valuable activities that would have helped me significantly in the years to come.

I had, unknowingly, established a series of limiting beliefs about my capabilities that affected many areas of my life. My unconscious strategy was little more than an attempt to avoid pain. If you've ever heard anyone say, "Don't expect too much or you'll be disappointed," you'll know what I'm referring to.

This way of thinking became deeply rooted and started to affect many other areas – perhaps *every* other area - of my life.

I'd much rather let others get into the action, just in case I made a mess of things and embarrassed myself. Even when I did step out to follow my passion for music, writing, teaching and team-building, they were usually not seen through to completion because of someone's pointed remark, somebody's 'well-intended' criticism or snidey comment.

I also found it hard to talk freely with girls whom I was attracted to, because I feared the potential rejection. Now that might be a pretty common occurrence, but for me it meant that many of these potentially rewarding relationships never even got started.

Looking back, I thought that one of my good points was that I had learned not to judge others by their background, their education, their skin colour or their abilities. All very noble, I thought, but even here there was a flip-side to this coin; if *I* was ever judged by another person it would send me into a complete tailspin and cause me inside pain for weeks.

So, with all this going on inside my head, of course there *were* many things I wasn't very good at – I didn't ever stick with anything long enough to *get* good at them.

Clearly I should have heeded the saying,

> *'No one ever got worse at anything*
>
> *by trying it one more time.'*

Occasionally, just occasionally, there were moments of praise and recognition for my achievements. For these I could be thankful and in them I could find a few nuggets of self-worth that helped me believe I was still capable of doing something well.

You must understand that, in my imagination, I had a long list of strengths. Unfortunately, these were not always easy to access in the real world.

So what was missing? Surely I had more resources available to me at these moments of challenge? So why couldn't I step up as I needed to?

The Tipping Point

This was the point at which I started my search for a way to access the resources that I truly believed lay dormant within me. Somehow I needed to bring this arsenal of abilities into play when I needed them most – to bring up the right card at the right time.

It's not that you don't need anyone else. No man, woman or child is an island. It's just that you have remarkable capabilities sitting on the bench just waiting to be called onto the pitch.

Just imagine having the ability to get yourself into the most resourceful, empowering frame of mind possible in any given situation. Would that transform the way that you went about things? Would that transform the results that you've been getting in life?

What I've come to realise is that there really is a highly capable team inside each one of us that is able to bring its abilities to the fore whenever the situation demands it.

No doubt about it

You are a team.

In these lessons we will also walk through some specific, practical exercises that will help you get in touch with character traits you've naturally subdued and learn to unleash their power at just the right moment. At the same time you will probably also encounter some character traits that you've naturally elevated a bit too high – and learn to tame those moods that sometimes get the better of you.

Now all growth involves some sort of stretching - which may not always feel comfortable at the time - yet I'm pleased to say that the great thing about the approach we're going to take in this course is that we're not going to be drumming up will power, repeating endless mantras or 'faking it til we're making it.' Instead, we will simply open a few doors to a whole team of resources that already exists inside us, a team that is ready to take action.

If you apply these lessons to your life I would expect you to experience what psychologists call a 'generative change' – a large-scale shift in your perception that affects multiple areas of your life at the same time.

The goal of any coach is not to build a following of readers and viewers, but of doers. So make up your mind now to put in practice anything that makes sense in your situation. Because, as you start to take real action, you'll join the elite ranks of those who have found themselves:

- Growing in confidence and gaining greater peace of mind
- Achieving greater recognition or even promotion at work
- Improving personal relationships
- Accelerating work team performance
- Increasing influence both professionally and socially
- Obliterating procrastination – having the motivation to take more direct action

These people have used this approach to gain a much greater insight into why they habitually do what they do and have learned to blast through limiting beliefs by accessing their own hidden capabilities.

If this is something you'd like to explore now, let's make a start.

Please see the next page and choose a hat...

*What kind of hat would you say you wear
most of the time?*

Do you see yourself as a bit of a warrior, or a joker; a lover
or a sage; a king, a queen or maybe a mystic?

We all recognise these characters; it's as if they have
existed in society since time immemorial. They are
prominent in the legends of old and we see them
perpetuated in numerous modern movies.

So what kind of person would you say you are? Which of
these characters would you identify with the most?

It's helpful to understand the specific role you play in life because the characters we reflect the most impact pretty much everything we think, say and do. It affects your approach to challenges, your degree of effectiveness at work, your methods of dealing with other people and also the way in which they relate to you.

This powerful truth is what you will be exploring as you journey through these lessons. I've seen many people's lives revolutionised as they've got to grips with this fact for themselves. The opportunity now lies before you to discover it for yourself.

But before we start to get too deep, let me take you to a foreign land, a long, long time ago...

"If you can step up,

<u>will</u> you now step up?"

CHAPTER 1 ~ Stepping Up

"Search for the hero inside yourself

Search for the hero inside

Search for the hero inside yourself

And then you'll find your reason in life."

M People

The Legend of Oakenthor

Scroll I

The King was dead.

Prince Sapler had been given the news that morning. He was rapidly escorted back to the palace and told he must address the people within the hour, changing, of course, out of his hunting gear and into more appropriate regalia to present reassuring words to his expectant subjects – words that were now being hastily scribed for him by some court official he had never met.

His father, King Oakenthor, had largely let him grow up alone in the royal household – attended to in every way by servants of many kinds, but not fathered. The King had clearly preferred to invest his time and effort into Sapler's older brother, Prince Ethan, and now both the King and the heir apparent lay dead at the bottom of a murky ocean with a platoon of bodyguards, the kingdom's chief negotiator and the wreck of a vessel legendary for its strength but fatally lacking sufficient means to bail nature's implacable waters.

Sapler's mother had died years before, when he was merely 7 years old. Something deep side the young prince had always pined for her company, her comfort and reassurance far more than his brother had ever seemed to show, but even his best memories of her were few and faded.

Memories of his father and elder brother, however, were now very present, swarming in his mind, each one jostling for prime place.

These men of renown had always been the capable ones, the strong ones, the valiant and noble ones for whose honour poems, odes and tapestries would be crafted by their loyal and awe-filled subjects. Even while they lived they formed the stuff of legends. His father was tough, decisive and savvy and he expected nothing less from his eldest son. His presence made the castle, indeed the entire realm, what it was. Together, this father and son stood as torches that lit the years to come; permanent pillars in the minds of the people; pillars of vision, wisdom and fortitude.

And then, in one sentence from a heavy-hearted aide, they had instantly become figures of the past. Oblivious to his fretful attendants, the anxious Prince Sapler managed to whisper, "Now there's only me. They are no longer a part of my future." That simple fact was the hardest thing to bear.

All this as it was, the present moment was now staring him in the face. Prince, soon to be *King,* Sapler was standing awkwardly before the bowing figures of courtiers, earls, and his father's five royal advisors – a solemn assembly of men and women he had barely spoken to in these 19 years of his life. He wished he could just get away to his private chambers for a while – a long while, if he had his way.

Of course, he *wouldn't* have his way; not now, maybe not ever. People would be placing uncomfortable demands upon him for the rest of his life. He was already feeling the crushing weight of responsibility for a kingdom that he'd always expected to leave in the hands of others far more capable than himself.

Walking passed the members of his sombre court, he thought he could read their eyes, 'He's not up to the task.' 'Still too young, still too careless.' 'The orphan King.' 'The unready King.' 'The couldn't-we-find-someone-more-suitable King.'

He clasped the speech in hand, ink still moist under a clammy palm. Then, putting on his bravest face, and praying that his voice wouldn't fail him for the next four minutes; he turned and walked to the balcony to address the waiting crowd.

Long live the King.

Mighty Oaks from Little Acorns Grow

Can you think of a time in your life when you did exactly the right thing? When you performed brilliantly and achieved things almost effortless results. Maybe you said just the right words at just the right time, drove yourself just a little more until the task was complete; connected with someone with whom others had given up; led a team on a successful mission or made a discovery that changed things for the better.

When such moments happen, something inside us seems to come alive - as if we've somehow managed switch into the right gear; releasing some kind of hidden energy that makes all the difference. Such events tell us that we were made for more than 'the same old', where so many people seem to live their daily lives.

Then what about those days when you know for sure that you could have done so much better?

You could have spoken out - but didn't. You should have finished it but you got distracted and then you simply ran out of time – leaving something important undone. You could have lent a hand. You should have paid more attention. You ought to have been able to work it out, but it was beyond you. With a bit more thought you could have planned things more effectively. In a better mood you would have chosen more appropriate words; taken better action, laughed it off, approached things differently.

So you know you're capable of better. Don't you?

> *"Put aside the Ranger*
>
> *– become who you were born to be".*
>
> Lord Elrond, in 'Return of the King'.
>
> JRR Tolkien.

Like muscles that have become weakened through lack of use, there are abilities inside you – inside everyone – that just need some gentle exercise and they'll come alive; they'll move, grow and begin to shape the world around them. Maybe you've heard someone coming out of a session with a personal trainer saying,

"He got me using muscles I didn't know I had!"

Well, that's exactly what we're going to be doing together through the course of this book, if... and it's a big if... you take action and actually do the exercises for yourself.

Facing the Challenge

How do you typically behave when confronted with a challenge? Different types of people respond in different ways, of course – typical ways, you could say. Let's go back to those characters we listed earlier – the hats; the roles we play in life.

If each of these characters found themselves in a specific set of circumstances you'd not be surprised if they each viewed their situation in very different ways. Because of this, each one is likely to propose a very different course of action to the others.

Imagine if some very bad news is reported to this crowd, how would you expect a king or queen to respond? How would a warrior react? What about a wise man or a jester? And how about a lover?

They would all see the situation from a different angle; they would focus on quite different aspects of the same event and so you'd expect them to behave quite differently from each other.

Archetypes

If you haven't heard of them before, I want to introduce you what the psychoanalyst Carl Jung referred to as 'Archetypes' (pronounced 'ark-uh-types').

Archetypes are simply models, or characters, that we would all recognise; who possess different perspectives, qualities and abilities.

Whilst there are many different archetypes that Jung and others have defined over the years, there are six particular ones that we're going to focus upon in this these sessions.

When you discover their distinctive traits you may well recall certain characters you have read about in stories, or heard about in legends or mythology. That's because they do each represent a 'classic' character type that would be recognised in pretty much every race and culture; language and creed. They are very much an ingrained part of our thinking as individuals and also in society at large.

The important thing to get to grips with, however, is that the defining traits of all these archetypal characters actually exist within every one of us - it's just that we naturally display some of these traits more often, and more intensely, than others.

As you get to grips with the concept of archetypes, it might be useful if I make plain that these are not separate *personalities* – there need be nothing schizophrenic about the fact that we house several different archetypes within. They are simply facets of what makes you, who you are. Like a diamond that has been cut to display many faces – each one reflecting light in a very specific way – there are many elements of our personal make up that light up more than others at certain times, and the ones that represent a group of related characteristics we're calling an archetype.

Once we understand these archetypes and learn to activate them in the right way, we will be able to evoke massive, positive change in situations that used to get too much to deal with.

At such moments of challenge we might need a significant boost of courage and determination, at other times we might need to be more compassionate or nurturing to get a result with someone. If you've ever looked back on a situation you know you could have handled better, this approach will provide you with a host of new resources.

It may be that you got hold of this book because you wanted to learn this approach less for yourself and more to help develop and improve the dynamics of a particular team that you're involved with. Because what you'll find is that archetypes have a significant impact on team dynamics.

Team Spirit

Every successful team is made up of people with different skills, perspectives and strengths. Recognising where certain people's personal strengths lie can help us build highly effective teams – whether on the football field or in the board room. You wouldn't want a hockey team full of goalies or a corporate board of only marketing directors. The differences in outlook and ability of each individual contribute to, rather than diminish, the team's strength and effectiveness.

A good leader ensures that accurate, timely knowledge is provided to her team. A great leader has already anticipated what each team member will do in response to that knowledge.

If you are a leader or a manager, how valuable do you think it would be if you had a method that:

A. Identifies specifically what motivates each member of your team, and
B. Predicts how each one would respond to any given challenge?

A successful outcome depends enormously upon these factors and such awareness would surely be a powerful asset.

Even if you're not actually a team leader, a coach or a manager of others, you may still find these dynamics very helpful when dealing with your family or any close-knit group of people.

* * *

Our assessment of others can be vitally important, but what about our perception of ourselves? Are you already aware of which archetypes are most dominant in your life? Do you understand which are weaker and could be holding you back? Or have you found that particular archetypes have a tendency to go a little overboard at times and become too much for others to handle?

Whatever anyone else has said or done to us through our lives, we are all ultimately responsible for the choices we make, the words we use, our responses, our behaviours and our actions.

The opportunity is now before us to leave the shadows behind and walk a road less travelled.

So who needs to step up now?

Who has to make this happen?

Team Me.

CHAPTER 2 ~ Identifying Your Archetypes

"Who are you? Who, who, who, who?"

The Who

The Legend of Oakenthor

Scroll II

The horseman drove hard. Scattering stones from the forest track his steed pressed on at his master's unrelenting command. He could see the castle now in the distance, displaying flags at half-mast; flags that drooped in the still, morning air; an air whose dampness seemed to pervade every tree in the woods, the stones of the dwellings, the minds of every king's subject.

The heavy gates were heaved open with a mournful creak as the messenger approached and closed behind him with a thud that spoke of duty and finality. He dismounted, ascended a short flight of steps and signalled to guards who gave him immediate audience with the king. With laboured breath and a furrowed brow, he delivered his urgent report.

"Your Majesty, I've heard from a reliable source that there was a meeting of the city's elders in Absalem last night. They are, right now, planning to break away from the kingdom and are already seeking support from the surrounding shires."

King Sapler felt a wave of shock pass through his mind and a draining of vitality from his body. Absalem was not only a highly fortified city, it was a prosperous port with a hinterland rich in natural resources, of timber and marble renowned across the known world, all of which would ensure they could finance their independent state indefinitely. But there was an added layer of personal betrayal in this conspiracy; the Earl of Absalem was his own cousin, Tyran.

Sapler felt weak, undermined, betrayed. He slumped back in his chair and stared at the floor wishing that his father was there to take command. Prince Ethan had often been given practice in this kind of thing. His father would quiz him about how he'd respond to all manner of challenging scenarios – testing and developing his abilities to assess situations and make decisions when the heat was on. Sapler had never been invited to join such conversations, and only caught a little of what they discussed as he played nearby. Ethan was the heir, the favoured one, so it was only right that he be trained this way.

But now Sapler had this kingdom thrust into his uneasy hands and, with no one to call upon for advice, his mind froze; stuck with the belief that whatever he did would likely be the wrong thing to do. Why couldn't he have an easy test in his first week as monarch?

"Your Majesty?" the messenger enquired with some urgency.

All Sapler could master was a weak, "Um, yes. Thank you. I'll..." but his words trailed to a blank. He didn't know what to do. Not at all.

"Should your armies make ready?" The messenger enquired, with not a little frustration. But Sapler said nothing. Then, trying to maintain appropriate respect for the Orphan King, the Unready King, he pressed more emphatically, "Should we not at least despatch spies, your Majesty?"

The messenger took a deep breath. He realised that hounding was not going to help and the new king needed some distinct support. "When your father faced a challenge that he was not immediately sure how to handle, he would call upon his counsel." he more gently proffered.

A curious look came across Sapler's face and he looked up. "His counsel? His royal advisors?"

"Yes, your Majesty – and more than mere advisors. These men and women were those your father relied upon not only for their insight on a range of matters, but also for their ability to carry out his bidding."

Within the hour the King's Counsel Chamber had been made ready. It was an elegant room at the eastern end of the castle, its walls covered with coats of arms and tapestries that depicted life in each of the shires and the battles they had fought against aggressive foreign powers and marauders from the Outer Isles. Four chairs were now filled around an oval table; there was a large, heavily decorated chair for the King and one further seat that remained empty.

King Sapler took his place at the head of the table and addressed the noble assembly before him.

"Prince Ethan was almost certainly better acquainted with you than I am," he started hesitantly; "I have to confess I only know some of your names. So, to make a start, can you each please tell me who you are and the role you played as an advisor to my father."

Immediately a broad man stood up, his military role clearly evident from his attire. "Well, you do know me, your Highn... your Majesty. I am Armadig, General of the King's Armies." He promptly sat down as if all that anyone needed to say had just been said.

The woman opposite Armadig was the next to stand and address the King. Her eyes seemed to embrace him with a motherly acceptance before any words had left her lips. "I am Freya. I have been reporting to the King on home affairs – all issues concerning our own people – for many years. After the untimely loss of Medattus, our chief negotiator, I have also assumed responsibility for all diplomatic relations with foreign powers."

As Freya took her seat, a lean man beside her with face engraved with lines of learning, of study and deep thought, stood and gave a slight bow. "And I am Sagitus, I have been the keeper of the royal archives for over 25 years. Your father would regularly seek my wisdom, reasoning and objective advice on matters of state, political strategy and details of our country's history."

As he concluded, he glanced towards an elegant lady in a deep crimson robe the other side of the table, who rose and faced the King to reveal her name. "Tekoia, your servant. I have responsibility over all matters of faith and spiritual wellbeing – directly regarding the royal household, but also across the realm."

Sapler noted the authority and gravitas of these people now seated before him. He felt that they were so much more capable, experienced and confident than he was, and his personal sense of inadequacy only increased. What had he ever achieved of any note? Yet, what chance had he ever been given? He grappled with the swirling cloud of dark, inner voices. Yet Sapler was no pretender. His honesty, they would all soon admit, was completely disarming and had an almost magnetic effect on those he spoke to.

"I have to admit that everything's happening a bit too fast for me to keep up with right now, so I am going to need to lean on you, as my father's advisors, to help me determine a best course of action as we tackle this troubling situation at Absalem."

He felt he should continue but Freya indicated she had something to add and politely interrupted, "There is another still to come, your Majesty."

Armadig rolled his eyes but said nothing.

A moment later there was a disturbance at the door. Into the room leaped a man dressed in the strangest of clothes and pockets stuffed with boxes, coloured handkerchiefs, dice, coins and all manner of other trinkets.

Hugo, the court jester bounded over to the fifth and final seat in the chamber. He made no excuse of any kind for being late and Sapler looked at him, rather bemused. He knew Hugo well enough, but was quite certain that this court jester was performing another one of his rather inappropriate practical jokes and interrupting what ought to be a serious meeting. He was about to ask his counsel who it was they were really expecting, when Tekoia stood once more, faced the King and formally annunciated, "Your Majesty, your counsel is now convened."

Identifying Your Archetypes

There is a team inside each of us that is ready to take on the challenges that each day may bring.

How well we perform in the face of these challenges will depend a lot upon how well developed each member of our team has become. Over the course of our lives, we will have quite naturally preferred some of our 'team members' over others, and the ones we've neglected, like under-exercised muscles, will naturally have become weaker.

Can you imagine how things would be for you now if you *had* managed things right, if you *had* stepped up at those moments of decision in your past?

So isn't it time now to call on the ones that have been sitting on the bench for too long; time got get them on the pitch to do what they do best.

So, here's a question,

If you *can* step up,

will you now step up?

Life can be trusted to send you an endless supply of disappointments, challenges, threats and bad news. Our choice is merely down to the way that we respond to each event. To ascend the heights, we need to see each challenge as an opportunity to rise further up; to become more. For it has been said that...

"If the mountain was smooth

You wouldn't be able to climb it."

Anon.

The Six Pack

You can find a good few books that build on Jung's Archetypes, or 'inner advisors' as some have called them, giving them various names and stressing the importance of particular ones over others. If you're familiar with the seminal works of Robert Moore and Douglas Gillette, and further applications by authors such as Jim Warner, you'll recall that they put their entire emphasis upon four essential archetypes: King, Warrior, Lover and Magician.

For my part, after many hours of coaching individuals to improve their personal and professional effectiveness, I've come to recognise the importance of two further, distinct characters that, together with Moore's Fab Four, I feel complete the circle of essential character traits that we all possess.

I am aware of several publications that speak of 12 archetypes, some 49 archetypes, and one that even identifies over 120 of them. Call me simple if you want, but I like to work with a 'six pack'; half a dozen foundational characters that make up my personal A-Team.

They are:

> The Sovereign
>
> The Warrior
>
> The Sage
>
> The Mystic
>
> The Lover
>
> The Jester

In all truth, I do recognise the place and value of a number of other key archetypes, but these are the six that I believe help us the most when it comes to performance improvement, both at home and at work.

There is a logic and balance in this model that will become much more apparent as we unpack the attributes and operations of these six archetypes and then explore how exactly they work together.

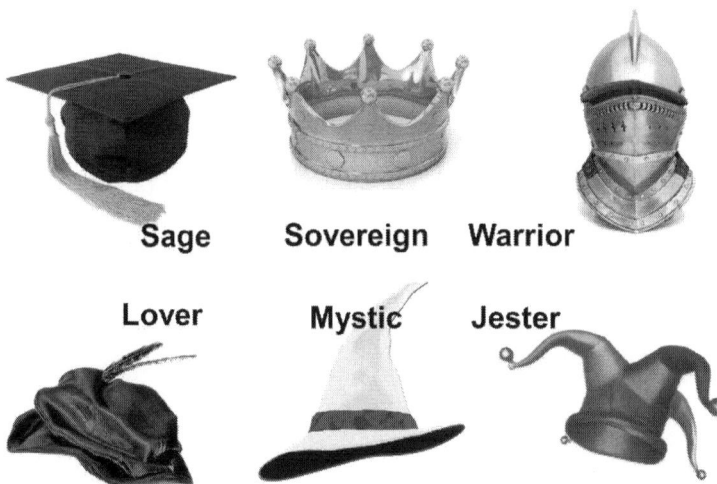

Sage   Sovereign   Warrior

Lover   Mystic   Jester

Horses for Courses

Of course these six characters exist almost entirely unconsciously for the vast majority of people but as we become more aware of them we will find just how distinctive they are.

So we should start by getting to grips with what it is that makes these characters so different from each other.

There are five important ways:

- They *see* things differently
- They *value* different things
- They establish different *priorities*
- They *act* differently
  (and therefore...)
- They get different *results* in life.

To put that simply: they behave in particular ways because they each have a different perspective on what's most important in life.

Giving a name to each of these archetypes is therefore only a start; we should now take a deeper look at each one in turn to find out what really makes them 'tick'.

The Sovereign (King or Queen)

Taking responsibility and assuming command are key traits of the Sovereign. Confident of their innate authority and their position of power, they direct the affairs of their realm to bring order and prosperity. They leverage the strengths and gifts of others in their team who can action the strategies that they create and communicate.

The Sovereign thinks that life is all about: having the power to establish order, justice, peace and prosperity for all.

The Warrior

Warriors take action and accomplish missions. They overcome challenges by using appropriate strength and determination, and are responsible for ensuring boundaries are enforced. They are skilled, capable and competitive; they stand up for themselves, are expressive and passionate, and prefer to work without too many dependencies on other people.

The Warrior thinks that life is all about: getting the job done.

The Sage

Clear understanding and factual insight mark the contribution of the Sage. Like Solomon of old, they esteem wisdom and knowledge; regarding learning as a vital part of everyday life. They are logical and astute and will search out the evidence until they arrive at the truth.

The Sage thinks that life is all about: continual learning and gaining accurate and superior knowledge.

The Lover

Lovers are trusting and open, even with people they've only recently encountered. They love creative expression and believe everyone has an intrinsic value. They nurture and seek harmony in every situation.

Valuing relationships and connection, Lovers are not just the Romeos and Juliets of the world; they are those whose primary focus is on other people.

The Lover thinks that life is all about: connection and harmony.

The Mystic

Mystics are very good at bringing transformation and managing change. Valuing faith, belief and dreams, they use their energy, charisma and an uncommon knowledge to influence people and situations. In this way they can be very powerful but they would rarely have the means to act by force or through raw authority.

Their detached viewpoint and awareness of the 'bigger picture' makes them stable during crises and good at mediation. They don't mind things being a bit ambiguous and they often have a rather different view of the best path ahead. Sometimes they will challenge or even break the rules.

The Mystic thinks that life is all about: making dreams come true.

The Jester

The Jester excels at finding the funny side to any situation. Refusing to get too serious, they share their light-hearted view of life with those around them – though not all would find this welcome.

They are colourful and playful, determined to live life like it's a game – boredom, rigidity and monotony will often spur them into action.

The Jester thinks that life is all about: making things fun.

There is a lot more that could be said about each of these archetypes but I'm imagining that you may already have found yourself identifying a little with one or two of these characters. So which ones would you say are the most influential in your own life; and which would you say usually take more of a back seat?

Because these characters are so accessible, so easy to recognise, and universal in nature, it may be no surprise to find that they often form the foundational characters of the myths and legends passed down through the generations of every culture in the world. These patterns are repeated by modern script-writers when developing their plots for everything from sit-coms to blockbuster movies.

Archetypes in the Movies

When it comes to Hollywood (and Bollywood), it seems that the bigger they want the blockbuster to be, the more archetypical they make their key characters; from the old Westerns to Star Wars; from Rocky to The Matrix. An epic example is The Lord of the Rings.

Lord of the Rings

In movie form, The Lord of the Rings trilogy is full of archetypal characters and whilst Tolkien's characters provided a solid foundation for each one, the script writers of Jackson's film trilogy exaggerated these archetypes even further. Here's a quick overview of the key roles in the story:

> **Aragorn** clearly represents the rising Sovereign. I say 'rising' because he first appeared as a bit of a loner, even an outlaw, known as Strider. As the story unfolds, we see him increasingly taking responsibility; making decisions, assuming command, initiating strategies, inspiring more and more followers, influencing the kings of other nations and finally taking his place as the King of Gondor.
>
> **Gimli** the dwarf is a classic Warrior. Always ready to fight for what's right; he is competitive, valiant, skilful and loyal; caring little about the odds as he launches himself into the fray.
>
> Wise and prescient, **Gandalf** clearly depicts the archetypal Mystic - a major agent of change. He often uses 'other-worldly' power to gain insights and perform feats that are beyond the abilities of the common man. His mere presence inspires hope amongst his beleaguered companions, and it is he who brought about King Théoden's transformation or 'exorcism' if you prefer.
>
> Quick to make light of every situation, the mischievous and playful Hobbits, **Merry** and

Pippin play the Jester's role. Have you noticed how the musical score changes whenever these two are centre stage in the first two films? It's also interesting to note that these characters were much less mischievous in Tolkien's original story but were developed this way in the films to provide a greater contrast between the key characters.

The Elves are then introduced as an entire race of mystic-type creatures. Yet what we see in the main character of **Legolas** is a mix of archetypes that imply he's clearly a leader in the making. Whilst remaining true to his Mystical elfish roots we also witness his skill, proactivity and athleticism as a Warrior. Added to these, he also showed some distinct traits of the Sage as he, in complete contrast to Gimli, typically sought to gain a true understanding of every situation before taking action.

And finally, we need to highlight the role the Lover depicted by the two heroines **Eowyn** and **Arwen**. These women are open, caring, impassioned, emotionally driven (hearts ruling heads), and whilst both have evidently focused their affections towards Aragorn, his preference is clearly set on the one who exhibits the more mystical qualities. A connection we'll be exploring later.

Of course, for most of the Lord of the Rings saga, Middle Earth was embroiled in a major conflict. Everyone in such a situation would need to call upon their Warrior nature to survive. Yet we can still clearly see a whole range of individuals in this story who each vividly represent a certain classic type of literary character; an archetype.

Moving away from Middle Earth, we should now head for Space; the final frontier.

Star Trek

Star Trek has been running since before even *I* was born. Still powering on after over 40 years on our screens, this modern myth must have some reason for its on-going success. Do you think it might be something to do with the prevalence of strong archetypal characters playing each of the major roles?

> **James Kirk** is the Sovereign in the pack, of course. He is the Captain, the strategist, the daring and commanding leader of the crew; responsible for all on the USS Enterprise.

> **Doctor McCoy (Bones)** is passionate and people-focused. His evident care and concern for others

places him clearly in the role of the Lover - even if he's a bit of a grumpy one at times. Noting his nickname, I think it interesting to note that the ancient Hebrews regarded the bones as the home of the emotions.

The Sage is most evident in the character of **Mr Spock**; the scientific officer who is always seeking detailed knowledge, examining the facts and investigating the evidence until he discovers the truth to any matter. Following the ways of his Vulcan ancestors he's obsessively guided by logic and reasoning (with not an emotion in sight). So he doesn't score highly on 'EQ' – the scale for Emotional Intelligence – and this is the primary cause of his frequent altercations with Doctor McCoy.

Though not portrayed as an aggressive man in any way, the chief engineer, **Scotty,** is probably the most evident Warrior-type on board the ship. He is action-orientated, direct, plain-talking, responsible and loyal in everything he does.

And if you wanted a more extreme example of the Warrior, you could always study the alien race known as the **Klingons.**

In J. J. Abrams' Star Trek of 2009, each of these archetypal characters was maintained without any significant embellishment or deviation. In Star Trek: the Next Generation series, new characters were added to introduce the dynamics of the Mystic and Lover. It's clear that the script-writers were working with classic character formulas in order to develop stories that would have a wide appeal.

Other Movies

The Warrior has always been a popular character in movies, just as they have been in ancient myths and legends.

Russell Crowe's character Maximus, in the film Gladiator, portrays a strong and classic Warrior. The movie starts with Maximus playing full-out as a hands-on, skilled, loyal and determined General in the Roman army.

Facing the subsequent murder of his family, however, he then becomes completely numb and passive; refusing to fight even when he's enslaved and given the role of gladiator. (We'll explore this 'frozen' state in some depth later.) It's not long before the fight returns to him however, and after many bouts in the arena he finds himself face to face with his arch-enemy; the Emperor himself. When the Emperor realises who he is, and provokes him to his face, Maximus answers as a highly matured Warrior; choosing to 'fight' not with his sword, but with some carefully chosen words saying, "The time for honouring yourself will soon be over."

Dr Who is very interesting character of modern myth who exhibits multiple, well-developed archetypes. Whilst it might be said that he has a strong leaning towards the 'left-brain' characters of the Sage, Sovereign and Warrior, he also expresses a good bit of Jester and more than a touch of the Mystic. And his internal struggle with the Lover has latterly been used to generate a stirring sub-plot.

Story-tellers though the ages have worked with tried and tested formulas that often focus upon one primary archetype whom they then surround with a number of clashing and complementary archetypal characters; both friends and villains. Like Spock and McCoy, the Sage-Lover clash is often evident, and have you noticed that where you find a Sovereign, you'll also invariably find a Mystic close at hand. The Mystic is not called upon for day to day matters, but when a crisis emerges; their few words can help steer an entire kingdom through a significant transition.

What we see performed on the big screen we also see acted out in real life. We resonate with these characters because they are already very familiar to us.

CHAPTER 3 ~ The Ancient Map

"I thought I told you, I'm a lover not a fighter."

Michael Jackson

The Legend of Oakenthor

Scroll III

Sagitus was the first to address the assembled counsel and the King leaned forward, eager to hear his views on how best to tackle the errant Absalonians. With his usual air of unhurried dignity, Sagitus proceeded, "I've been weighing the merits of allowing the Absalonians a greater degree of independence – I think there would be much benefit in negotiating..."

"Negotiating? What!?" interjected an indignant Armadig, "With those rebellious, conniving fools?" Armadig had bolted up with such a force that he had sent his chair backwards, toppling it onto the cool stone floor. Oblivious to the damage he was causing and leaning into the table like a gated bull, he continued, "We should go in hard; capture or kill the Earl and his treacherous henchmen and establish martial law until we are sure the revolt has been completely stamped out!"

Freya's voice was no less passionate, but with a different tack she quickly responded. "Whilst they've clearly erred in this matter, it's also true to say that they have been neglected of late. I can understand their need to stand up for themselves regarding the recent import levies. They evidently want to be heard – and I'd be happy to lead a delegation as Sagitus has suggested."

Armadig hated the very word 'delegation' but, for once, he thought it best to hold his peace until the others had presented their views. He muttered something under his breath and sat down to await his moment.

Tekoia then calmly motioned with her hand. The counsel were used to this strange sign that brought every eye in the room towards her and caused an expectant hush to descend upon all around – even upon the King himself. She spoke slowly and purposefully, as if repeating words she was receiving in some sort of vision. "Earl Tyran has had a long-standing feud with the woodsmen of Arboritum. The dispute is over the tolls he imposed on the roads that lead to the northern port. Support them and we could create a valuable ally in this struggle."

"We're just pussy-footing around!" Armadig insisted, disregarding his earlier constraint. "A bunch of old carpenters aren't going to solve this problem. We need a fighting force." He turned to the King hoping that at least he would show better sense – at least the sense to follow the advice of his father's loyal and experienced General. "The army is ready to march on your command, your Majesty."

There was a moment of silence. It was a silence that had, in days past, provided King Oakenthor room to probe the proposals being heard, challenge the assumptions, or announce his decision. Only the new, young King Sapler remained quiet; still weighing what was said, quite unsure how to manage the conflicting opinions of men and women far more experienced than he in the affairs of state.

It was at this point that Hugo pulled out a large spinning top and launched it before them on the table, a table whose surface was as smooth as marble; the craftsmanship, as everyone present could not have failed to notice, of the renowned Arborians.

The maverick had said nothing up until now. In fact he'd done little but amuse himself with a small box that appeared to be a kind of puzzle made of wood. But now it was he whom had the attention of the whole room as he gazed at his spinning device and gathered his words.

The General was never particularly patient with Hugo. In his eyes he was a fool whose only value was in entertaining the troops during days away from active service. But even he realised that a further outburst would do no good.

"The answer," Hugo suddenly announced, "is clearly… in the wood." Some eyes went to the wooden top, some to the table; some even glanced around for his strange puzzle. Armadig simply rolled his eyes upwards in exasperation.

Continuing, as if all present would want nothing better than to hear him perform, he riddled, "Catch the deviant Earl unawares. He visits the shrine in the glade of Silvanius without fail on the morning of the seventh day. Go early to the wood; to the south, where it meets the toll road, and seize him whilst he prays."

Sagitus didn't like it much when the jester tried to speak like an oracle yet he saw the synergy between Tekoia's observations and Hugo's poetic plan. Assessing the implications, he added what he saw as the logical conclusion. "If we do gain the woodsmen's support we could seize the toll gates with ease. It would cut off one of his greatest sources of materials not to mention income, and provide us with some valuable allies in the game. And I think we're likely to have similar success with the quarrymen. "

Hugo looked ever so smug as he concluded. "We will have captured their leader and cut off a vital supply line to the city. I'd just love to see his face when that happens." he chuckled.

Sapler knew it was now down to him to make a decision. He saw how each one of his advisors had brought a different facet of understanding to the situation. A number of these could now be combined to form a more robust plan of action but other input, notably that from Armadig, would have to be ignored, and he wasn't sure he wanted to face the consequence of that.

All fell still. The counsel awaited his word.

Your Personal Archetype Profile

Leaving the mythical stories and psychological theory aside for a bit, we should now start to get practical and personal.

You're about to create your own, personal archetype profile.

By now you may have a sense that you would like some of these archetypes to become a little more developed in your life; that you need to step up and grow to become a person of greater character. You may have a vision of what that person looks like; you may have seen others who display the characteristics you want to adopt yourself.

So the first thing we need, if we're going to develop and utilise the archetypes within us, is a personal map – a simple chart with a scale of measurement to show us where we really are.

Why is this profiling important? When you gain a greater sense of self-awareness you are able to identify and address the issues that have been holding you back. This in itself is no guarantee that you will change, grow or develop in any way, but it provides you the crucial first step – a picture of where you really are.

Without such a map, it will be unclear what's driving you and also what has been causing you to sabotage your own plans and dreams. How then could you make any adjustments? How could you take any intelligent action?

So, here's a simple exercise you can do right now on a bit of paper. Whilst my private clients and those who attend my workshops get a lengthy questionnaire that provides them with a much more precise view of things, you can still get a reasonably accurate indication from your simple gut feeling.

A very simple diagram can be used to develop a profile of the six archetypes and their degree of influence in your life. Along the bottom row you simply list each of the archetypes by name: the Sovereign, the Warrior, the Sage, the Mystic, the Lover and the Jester.

Above each you draw a vertical scale from 0 to 10.

To complete the profile, you do need to know the characteristics of each archetype, so you might want to remind yourself of these by reviewing the descriptions provided earlier.

Then, all you need to do is:

1. Ask yourself how much you express the key traits of each of these archetypes

2. For each archetype, place a mark somewhere between 0 and 10 to indicate how strong you think each one is. So if you think you have dominant Warrior tendencies, then you would choose a 7, 8 or even a 9 for that one. If you think you're not very brainy, you'd probably indicate a lower score, maybe a 2, 3 or maybe a 4 for the Sage. You do this for each of the archetypes; putting a number against each of their names.

So do this right now. We will be referring back to it later.

Your Archetype Profile

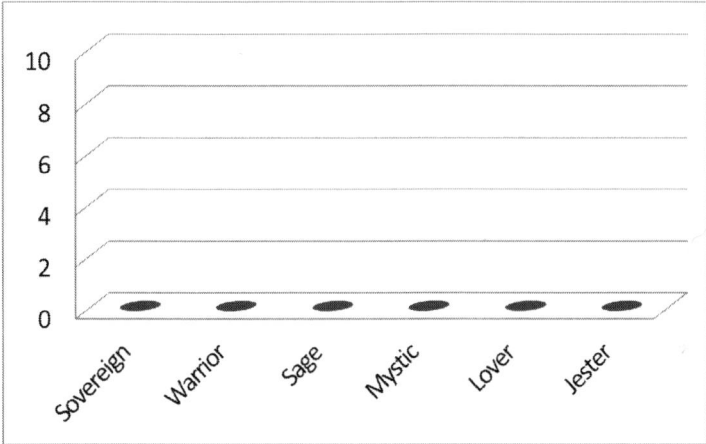

Now that you've done this, take a moment to look now at your results.

I'd be interested to know if this exercise has already revealed anything new to you. I find that as my clients and workshop delegates fill this out for the first time, some find it incredibly revealing – gaining a new perspective on who they are and why they do what they do.

Others find no particular surprises and simply agree that it reflects how things are. For these people, the significant (even life-changing) understanding often comes as we compare their profiles to the requirements of their current job, or maybe against the expectations of their spouse, partner or friends and family. Because that's very often where the rubber meets the road.

Does your job require more of the Warrior than you feel you have inside? Does your boss want to see more of the Sovereign? Does your spouse, girlfriend or boyfriend want to see more of the Lover or Jester in you?

So ask yourself if you're happy with what you see in your own profile. Take a moment to seriously consider the following questions:

- Is there an area that you think is a little out of balance - either too *strong* for your role in life, or too *weak*?
- Has any one of these traits got you into trouble at times?
- Which would you wish to see developed further?
- If you score very high as a Warrior or Sage, how fulfilling are your relationships with others?
- If you scored low as Sovereign, has this trait cost you something to let others make most of the decisions in your life? I suspect that in some way it will have.
- If you scored very high on Mystic, would you say that you have difficulty achieving many tangible results?

It's true that I'm making a few generalisations here but the patterns are really very common.

Whilst completing your profile, you may have wondered if you might have given very different answers on another day or in a few months' time – and you'd probably be right. That's because our changing environments do draw out different traits from us. So you can do this exercise as often as you want to and, whatever situation you find yourself in, will discover which areas need an extra bit of attention.

* * *

Helping you *get out of stuck* really just involves three simple steps:

1. Identifying the relative strengths of the six archetypes in your life using the archetypes profiling tool.
2. Identifying the archetypes that are required to tackle the challenge ahead of you.
3. Helping you step into the character of the archetype you need in greater force until it becomes a natural part of the way you do things.

To enable this last step, I would usually ask you to find a time when your required archetype was taking a leading role and guiding your behaviour. If you can recall any such time, even if not directly related to your current challenge, I would lead you in a couple simple techniques to help you to bring the energy of that past event into the present and begin to influence your current situation for the better.

At the same time I might also need to help you 'tame' some over-exercised character traits. This can happen when an archetype becomes too dominant in your life and starts to cause damage to those around it.

We'll have more on these techniques later.

* * *

Have you wondered how character issues might affect your choice of career?

Choosing your Career

It will be no surprise to find that people who exhibit certain dominant archetypes will be predisposed towards particular job roles or careers.

Corporate CEOs, Mayors and Captains of sea-faring vessels all need to have strong Sovereign traits – setting the course ahead and making decisions that their various managers and deputies will carry out; matters that affect all those within their care.

Sages may become teachers, lawyers, professors, detectives, technicians, accountants or quantum physicists; roles that demand specific knowledge, a detailed grasp of the related facts and a clear understanding of the issues at hand. Sages would also be found in consultancies, but here they would need to combine their specialist knowledge with the tenacity of a Warrior that would enable them to complete and deliver their projects and reports – often with little support from others.

Athletes must have the Warrior's discipline, drive and competitiveness; the Police need to use the Warrior's determination to enforce the boundaries of the law; construction workers and project managers need the Warrior's skill, focus and resilience to work the plan and overcome whatever challenges crop up along the way.

Even a nurse, with his strong requirement for Lover will at times need to operate in his Warrior in order to do whatever is required to support and even save the life of his patient.

Mystics, with their love for transformation, often find their place in research and development, in change management and coaching.

Managing a hotel kitchen requires a mix of Warrior and Lover ...with a little bit of Sage (if you can excuse the double entendre).

There are very few job roles that would demand from you the strengths and abilities of only one mature archetype. More usual would be the need for a combination of at least two or three archetypes that together would enable you to do the job well. From task to task you're likely to find a different archetype is leading your thinking and behaviour.

The Flip Side

We should also be aware of which characters would *not* make a good fit when it comes to certain professions. If you were running a business, you would never want to hire a Mystic to manage your finances, nor a mature Sovereign as a cleaner. You'd be asking for trouble if you were to employ a Warrior in a diplomatic role or to hire a Jester as a data analyst – that really *would* be a joke!

In the face of crisis there is a very real need for leaders who are familiar with the ways of all of the archetypes; those who are able to not only lead their teams of diverse characters but also be capable and willing to step into the role of any lacking part themselves.

Let's look at a couple of example situations where the attributes of various archetypes can be seen to result in both positive and negative outcomes.

A few months ago I interviewed a lady who worked as an educational manager in the UK prison service. It became clear that she felt she was a little too strong on the Warrior side and needed to develop her Lover a lot more. Dealing daily with adult offenders requires the continual reinforcement of boundaries, so the Warrior is rightly the archetype that you'd expect her to bring to the fore. Yet it was also clear that she felt she was losing touch with her nurturing nature and wanted to reclaim it; believing that those under her care would benefit from the more understanding and supportive facets of her temperament. What was also interesting to note is that this lady had two academic degrees – which would make her pretty bright by most peoples' standards - and yet when she completed her archetype profile she gave herself a score of only 2 or 3 for the Sage. I asked her why she gave herself such a low score in this area when she had two degrees. She answered, *"Oh you don't need to be very bright (like a Sage) to get a degree - you just have to be determined and keep at it until it's done."*

That's the talk of a Warrior, of course.

The Arabian Knight

A notable example from military history is T. E. Lawrence (known to many as Lawrence of Arabia) who led the Arab Revolt against the Ottoman Empire in 1916-18. You may think that such a man would clearly demonstrate some strong Warrior and even Sovereign traits, yet when you read the account of his antics it becomes clear that he approached things far more from the position and viewpoint of a Mystic.

Lawrence's influence and charm was strong enough to unite squabbling Arab tribes and, challenging the prevailing wisdom of both the local and the military authorities, led them in their first significant military victory; the capture of Aqaba. This was an impressive feat which earned him an instant recognition and promotion, yet his blasé approach to a subsequent mission led him straight into captivity. He had no plan, no back-up, just a belief that he'd be able to overcome whatever odds he faced by having faith in his own powers and 'playing it by ear' until he succeeded. Only this time he was captured, imprisoned and even tortured. The pain of this episode will certainly have caused him to review his faith in a purely a mystical approach to things.

If you think about it, what you'll discover is that the archetypes you've developed the most over the course of your life are the ones that you've been rewarded for the most – the ones that have regularly brought you the best outcomes.

Train of Thought

Ask yourself how you would act in this situation...

I was boarding a train recently with a large number of other passengers who were journeying from London to Manchester. I noticed a man had sat down in his reserved seat at a table close by. He pulled out a book and a laptop and started work. Soon enough three women appeared together, evidently having tickets for the other three seats around the same table. After all the expected shuffling and settling, one of the women turned to the man and in a strong French accent said, *"May I ask something quite horrible?"*

"Certainly, what is it?" The man replied, giving her his full attention.

"Could you please just go somewhere else?" she said.

Now what would you have said or done in his position?

Note for a moment your instinctive response, and then begin to ask how each of our six archetypes might have dealt with things.

Think of how a Warrior would likely have reacted in the face of such a question, and then how a Sage might have responded. Would a Jester have said something different to a Lover?

The train carriage was now very full but he didn't glance around even for a moment. Other passengers around them were starting to notice what was happening and began to watch with interest.

The man simply let out a relaxed and confident laugh. He showed no sign of offense, irritation or intimidation at all but with a smile, that seemed to come through his eyes, not just across his lips, he seemed to radiate a calm presence that began to positively affect those around him. The woman's rather embarrassed companions tried to make excuses for her, *"We're sorry, she always has to have everything just her way. You don't need to move."*

Then, looking directly at his provocateur, the man replied without any hint of annoyance, *"Oh, I have no problem with you asking such a thing. However, I also have no problem saying, 'Actually, no.'"*

One of her companions followed this remark by saying, *"Then you must be a very centred individual."* Which the gentleman acknowledged with a silent smile, as a centred individual would, and all four of them continued in pleasant conversation for a while after. I even heard one of the 'bossy' woman's colleagues saying later, *"I think she now finds you quite attractive and wouldn't want you to go away."*

To me this man seemed to have achieved a rare balance. The Sovereign was very evident in his demeanour; for he was clear where his boundaries lay and, as a mature Warrior, he had no hesitation enforcing them without any hostility or malice.

The Lover he expressed ensured that his provocateur was initially heard and was then in no way chastised or belittled though her request was clearly refused. And the Jester was present enough to take the woman's request lightly; peppering the on-going conversation with humour which built rapport and defused any vestiges of offense.

* * *

Vivre la Difference

We should make it clear that the aim of studying and developing these archetypes is not for us to each attain a '10' for every archetype in our profile, rather it is to gain a better understanding of our personal tendencies and gain a greater awareness of the traits that, whether by nature or nurture, have become the primary drivers of our behaviours. This way, we can intentionally contribute our unique strengths to any team that we have joined.

In a team setting, our differences as individuals can become our corporate strength – if, that is, each character is willing and able to work together.

At the same time we should also acknowledge that there is value in seeking to develop all six archetypes to a high degree. To have achieved this, and to have the presence of mind to employ their various strengths productively at any given moment, is a sign of a true leader.

The Call to Leadership

If you are in a position of leadership, or are heading towards such a role, then you may find that traits of the Sovereign have been coming to the fore over time. Of course this does need to be well developed if you are to lead, to direct others, to establish and fulfil a vision. And at the same time, it is vital that you know which advisors to call upon when you face each challenge that appears. If you take time to identify and develop those areas in you that are weaker, then you'll fare much better. The most effective leaders in the long run must be all-rounders.

As a lesson from history, Winston Churchill played a magnificent role as a Warrior-Politician before and during WWII. At that time he was exactly what the nation needed. Yet after the war he was quickly replaced by voting Britons because they realised that a warrior was not what they needed now that military objectives were no longer a focus.

* * *

Have a look at the following profiles and ask yourself whom would you prefer to have as a leader: A or B?

Archetype Profile - Leader A

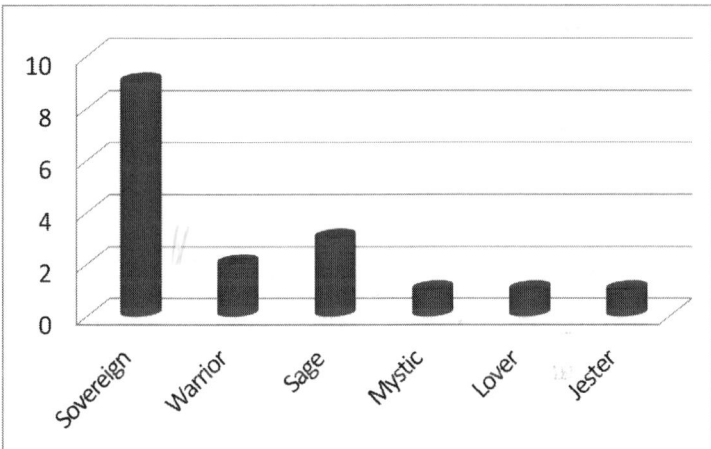

Archetype Profile - Leader B

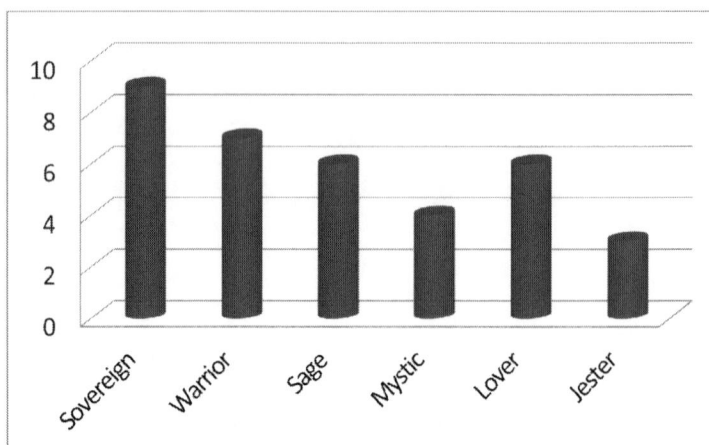

Can you explain your answer?

What have we learned so far?

We all have an inner team, a counsel of personal advisors who, by their relative influence in our lives, shape our perspectives on life and therefore influence (even control) the way we feel about things – motivating us in everything we do and influencing the way we do it.

These archetypes may be represented in numerous forms, but the Team Me approach focuses on a specific set of six that I've found to be the most useful in gaining valuable leverage, especially when it comes to personal and professional development, to change an individual's response to any challenge they face.

These archetypes are not split personalities, or 'parts' as Neuro Linguistic Programming (NLP) practitioners might call them, but unconscious models of thought, concepts that organise our thinking, characters that we all recognise.

Though these archetypes may be little more than metaphors, their influence on our behaviours can be monumental. When we learn to tap into their various strengths, we find resources that can significantly change our approach and enable us to overcome numerous, previously insurmountable obstacles.

Often it's their combined strengths that are required to manage the challenge at hand.

But how exactly do you strengthen those areas you realise need to be developed? How can we get ourselves to grow?

CHAPTER 4 ~ Developing Your Archetypes

"Just between us

I think it's time for us to realise

The differences we sometimes fear to show.

Just between us

I think it's time for us to recognise

The spaces in between

Leave room

For you and I to grow."

Rush

The Legend
of
Oakenthor

Scroll IV

King Sapler wasn't so certain about the plan that was emerging. He saw some merit in it and four of his five advisors seemed to be backing it, at least in part, but to him it still appeared incomplete.

Leaning forward now, though still with little confidence, he said, "If we can capture Tyran, all well and good but he'll be expecting some form of retaliation from us, and if our plan fails..."

He felt an increasing tightness at the top of his chest and hesitated once more. He knew it was now down to him to take ultimate command and responsibility, but it all felt so unnatural; nothing was giving him the confidence he'd seen in his father. Uncomfortable, yet knowing that to say something would be better than saying nothing, he started to query the outcome this plan might achieve.

"If our plan to capture him fails, all we'll have gained is some disruption to their supplies of wood and stone – and, yes, with it an impact on his revenues. But this is all too long term. We need a swifter resolution."

Armadig settled a little easier into his seat, pleased with the direction this was going, yet it was Tekoia who followed his point, "Whatever our course of action, your Majesty, timing is everything. We must act now before he has time to organise and cover his vulnerabilities."

"Then we must at least start the dialogue with him – request we meet on neutral ground and show we're ready to talk. We must appear fair, not brutal." Freya insisted, glaring at Armadig.

Sagitus was nodding as he added, "The way you act now, your Majesty, will determine the support of your people in the years to come."

"I've said what needs to be said," said Armadig, bluntly. "The army is ready to take him on directly, your Majesty. My troops match his three to one."

King Sapler paused for a moment. Whilst he needed their advice, he couldn't help feeling that these advisors were still being a little patronising towards him. This was the place, however, where decisions had to be made; there was nothing to do but to weigh their words and take the responsibility of command with a final, sovereign decision.

He acknowledged again that old tightness in his chest, yet this time it was as if he spoke to it, saying, "I realise you're really just wanting my protection, but indecision isn't any form of protection now is it?"

As he said this to himself, he felt something released inside and he was suddenly free to meet the demand of the moment. With a new sense of poise, he drew his conclusion.

"It appears we have some diverse opinions about the best way forward." His stating of the obvious actually helped in no small way to settle the atmosphere in the room. Tekoia gave a slight smile at this and became curious as to what the King might say next.

"We do need a rapid conclusion and that's only going to happen if what we engage in is well planned.

"Freya, send word to Earl Tyran that we wish to talk. Offer to station a tent on the plains of Mara Perez in two days' time where negotiations can be conducted. Whilst we await his reply, Armadig, I need you to work with Sagitus to devise a way of capturing Tyran before he reaches the shrine tomorrow morning."

A rare, mental image of his own father in action suddenly flashed through the young King's mind and Sapler added, "Any questions?" with an uncharacteristic gravitas.

No questions were uttered, so the King rose, rapidly followed by each of his counsel, who did not fail to discern the change that had just occurred before them.

As the meeting was adjourned, Freya immediately briefed her most trusted messenger and Tekoia joined Sapler outside on the battlements. She was curious about the change she had just witnessed but, as he surveyed the sun-drenched plains before them, she had another matter on her mind. "We had wondered why you hadn't called for any of us until the Absalem incident." She ventured. Seeing his openness to her enquiry, she continued, "Your father would call upon us regularly – though often not altogether. He'd often want to get our views on one matter or another, else entrust us with a specific task or mission to complete."

The King recalled his years of youthful isolation as his brother progressed through a structured programme of royal training. "I simply didn't know how things were done, Tekoia. I never had his guidance in matters of any real significance."

Tekoia was eager not to dwell on the past and sought to keep the counsel as the subject of conversation. "It is true that we seldom agree on anything, at least not initially," she added, "but your father would weigh our various contributions and make his final decision."

Standing a little closer to the young king, she offered a further suggestion. "We are all here to provide our advice whenever you need us. Yet I think you will find that, once you've heard our counsel in a number of different situations, you will begin to absorb something of our perspectives, even of our abilities, as your own. Soon you will be hearing our counsel inside you, and you will find that you can identify the best course of action yourself."

As Sapler looked down from the ramparts on to the market stalls and the rooftops of the village houses below, an idea came into his mind that caused his countenance to brighten, and Tekoia was curiously reminded of a youth she once saw preparing to board a galleon of adventure and discovery.

"Then I shall immerse myself in the ways of each of you," he said with a hurried anticipation, "even into Hugo's world of folly. I will live with you each in turn. I'll follow you, talk with you, eat with you... and see what I might learn from your varying perspectives on life. Then I'll see through your eyes and hear through your ears and gain for myself many ways of interpreting any situation."

Pleased to see this new hunger for wisdom, a hunger not dampened by the indecision she'd seen so much of before in the young prince, Tekoia simply replied, "We will assist you in every way we can, my King."

Developing Your Archetypes

Thus far we have established that each of us unconsciously plays host to a number of archetypes in our minds. Some of these archetypes are naturally stronger than others in their influence on our perspectives and behaviours.

When you first start to identify your own natural archetypal strengths and weaknesses you may discover an opportunity for further growth and maturity.

This might be because you've discerned that certain areas of weakness are actually hampering your career, your progress at work, your most important relationships (or lack of them), or social life or your general sense of fulfilment.

If this is the case then you may want an effective way to address the areas that you've identified and so these next few sections have been designed to guide you through some specific ways of doing just that.

Using a Role Model

Probably the fastest method of learning the ways of these archetypes is not by reading about them, though that can help, it's to get alongside someone who exhibits their characteristics. Doing this with someone you respect, quite simply and naturally causes something to 'rub-off' on you.

Over the past century, the idea of an apprenticeship as a way of learning a trade has become virtually forgotten. The more recent resurgence of *mentoring* may be helping to redress this imbalance a little but what we need most of all is to spend time with those who are already succeeding in those areas of life that we want to see developed in ourselves.

But would they happily invest their valuable time to do this with us?

I've been running internship programmes for many years and have seen college graduates enormously enhance their skills, capabilities and awareness of the industry, which puts them leagues ahead of those who have merely been taught in classroom settings. Even in a very tough job market I've seen many of these interns go straight into executive roles in their chosen field. In return, the company gets many hours of help at a vastly reduced cost. It's a win/win situation, a mutually beneficial arrangement. What these interns have done by choosing to learn about a specific industry, you can do by choosing to learn from someone with a strong archetypal make up that you know you are lacking.

Of course, if you're already in full time employment, starting again on an internship may not be an option for you. But there's more than one way to get close to those whose input you need.

Make it a priority to find and learn from someone who can strengthen you in any area where you lack; to provide you with an inspiring example that you can model, to warm what has become frozen inside of you and to cool those characteristics that may have become a little over-active in your life.

Trace Element

There was a time when it was clear that I needed to see a significant improvement in the sales of training programmes I'd been running. I'd always left the sales task to others, but the current system simply wasn't working well enough.

Realising that I could not lead others where I myself had not travelled, I determined that I would learn the ropes myself and, for a time at least, spearhead an approach that would work for our company.

But what I have to stress is there was a reason I'd avoided 'sales' up until that point; I really didn't feel comfortable doing that sort of thing. I'd always regarded sales-people with a fair degree of suspicion and would much rather spend my time refining products than trying to sell them. At this point in time, however, this was not an option. We needed sales quickly and someone had to take a lead.

It has often been stated that, 'When the student is ready the teacher will come.' At this point in my professional life, this was exactly how it was, because the very week that I made my decision to step up, I was invited along to a 3 day event where Brian Tracy was teaching on Leadership, Management and *Sales*.

I went to the seminars, I took copious notes and on one day, along with a number of others, even had a chance to lunch with the man himself.

After the event I bought several of Brian's CD series. From then on, he was with me when I was jogging, washing up, driving and commuting on the train. I learned many, many new things from this man who made the sales process sound much more simple and natural than I'd ever expected.

More than that though, even though I was only physically present with him for a short time, something intangible rubbed off on me, and it has stayed with me ever since. I immediately started building a better list of sales leads, writing sales scripts, making calls, improving our promotional materials and taking more consistent action to follow up on leads.

Many of these things were alien to me just a month before and have now become a natural part of what I do. It felt like I hadn't just changed gear – I felt I'd received a completely new gear box.

You can experience the exact same shift if you spend time with people who exhibit those desirable archetypal traits that you know you need. You can get it from their books, from listening over and over to their teachings and watching them on video – even if you never get a chance to meet them in person.

I'm so thankful for the internet in this regard, because you and I can get the materials we need in a matter of minutes, in pretty much whatever format we want. Quite simply, we have no excuse.

The Power of One

The wonderful thing about these archetypes, is the fact that even though they might be dormant, they are all already in us – already a part of our character.

Though I fully recommend learning from someone who can be an archetypal role model, we don't have to wholly rely on others to help us grow and mature in each area of need. We can do a lot to develop these archetypes by activating them ourselves – exercising them like a physical muscle so that they grow in capacity and become stronger. Once we've done that we can ultimately call upon their strengths whenever required.

<u>WARNING</u>

THE FOLLOWING EXERCISE MAY

SERIOUSLY ALTER

THE COURSE OF YOUR LIFE.

Please give it the time it deserves.

Exercise

So, before we go further, complete the following sentences:

1. The two most important archetypes I need to see developed in my life are:

    1._____

    2._____.

2. The specific people I could look to as examples to follow are:

    1._____

    2._____.

3. Three specific actions I'm going to take right now to progress in this are:

    1. _____

    _____

    2. _____

    _____

    3. _____

    _____

I have to mention here that, with or without a role model to help you learn the ways of these key archetypes, you should probably take a moment to hear my unique Archetype Activation Audios that I've specifically designed to strengthen each of the archetypes as you choose. The words, music and voice tone literally stir up the characteristics of each archetype within you – just as seeing a strong movie character portrayed on film can awaken and strengthen certain character traits within you – whether they are positive or negative.

Make sure you listen to the samples at: www.teamme.com/products

In our journey to understand how these archetypes operate we should now explore some deeper layers of their characteristics and behaviours. As we do this we'll discover that each one has a unique set of values – the things they regard as most important in life – and from these values, each has a unique set of perspectives.

Perspectives

A perspective is simply the *way* that somebody looks at something. In a meeting someone might ask, "What's your angle on this? How do you see it?" or, in a debate, a chairman might ask for different *viewpoints* on the subject being discussed.

To explore some of the unique perspectives that each archetype maintains, we can simply choose a subject (a big, broad subject often works best) and ask ourselves how each archetype would view that subject.

Because of their differing values and beliefs about things, each archetype then has a set of 'filters' through which they view any and every subject in life; whether it be knowledge, money, time, people, humour, music, energy... the list can go on.

Have a look at how each archetype might respond a prompt like: 'Tell me about knowledge.'

The Sovereign

"Knowledge is essential to make wise decisions that will prosper my realm."

The Warrior

"Clear knowledge is essential for making quick decisions and taking action."

The Sage

"People die from a lack of knowledge. Knowledge is therefore the key to life."

The Mystic

"There is a deeper knowledge that few ever learn to access."

The Lover

"Knowledge helps us better connect; to understand each other, to share."

The Jester

"The love of knowledge is the root of all wit. Better knowledge begets more fun in life."

Notice how each of these characters immediately links the subject at hand with the things that are most important to them – their highest values. If you hadn't seen which one was doing the talking, do you think you would have been able to identify the archetype by their response alone?

As you get familiar with each character this becomes increasingly easy and you'll start to understand which archetypes are the most dominant in those you're listening to.

Whether developed through nature or nurture, your unique personal perspective on life will steer everything you think, say and do. Every psychologist will be aware of how our minds delete, distort and generalise the information we're receiving through our five senses.

Whilst these profoundly influential processes are going on all the time they are happening at an almost entirely unconscious level. The vast majority of us have no idea why we prefer things a certain way, why we see things differently to others, why we value different things in life or why we find ourselves being attracted to certain activities, jobs or even types of people.

Understanding your dominant archetypal qualities will go a long way to explain these things.

* * *

As you get more and more familiar with archetypes you might begin to discern another vital dynamic that is very common between people; because each of these archetypes has a *complementary opposite*.

Poles Apart

You might have noticed in everyday life that someone who is predominantly led by the archetype of the Lover (who has a strong desire for connection and harmony), often seems to be drawn to someone who strongly exhibits the Warrior archetype (who seeks challenge and competition). This might initially be completely unexpected as, on the surface of things, their values and preferences are really at odds with each other. Once you become aware of it, however, you're likely to start seeing this dynamic reflected in numerous personal and professional relationships.

This mutual attraction doesn't mean that they always find each other easy to get on with – sometimes there can be fireworks between them. But despite their evident differences, they often seem to have an admiration, a fascination and at times even a boundless desire for their counterpart type.

Remember the old adage that '*opposites attract*'. When we look at these Archetypes, this saying certainly holds true.

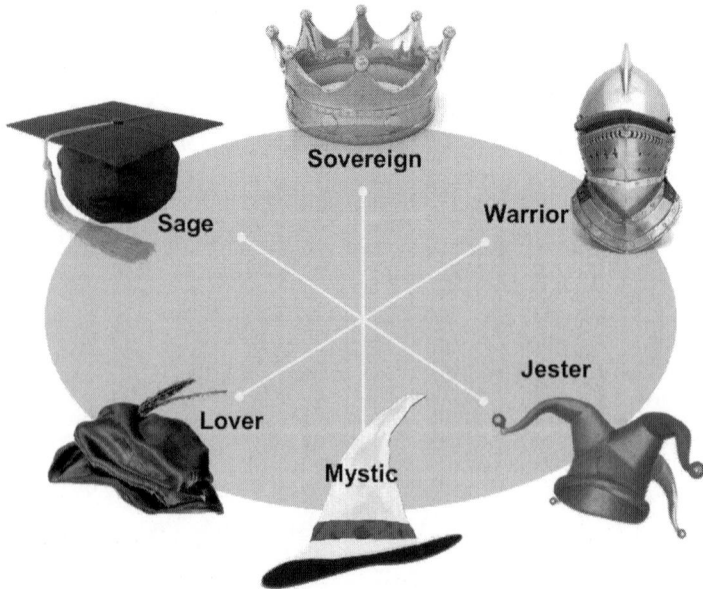

Complementary opposite Archetypes

So we find that the Warrior, for all his toughness and resilience, longs to find comfort in the arms of an adoring Lover; and she in turn admires the strength and tenacity in him that she feels she lacks, and yet still needs, herself.

Likewise the Sovereign knows that she can make things happen by her mere command - utilising her position of authority - yet she has an admiration for the Mystic who is also able to make things happen but does so, almost magically, through his belief and influence.

The Sage may often not 'suffer fools gladly' yet he can appreciate the perceptive wit of the Jester and benefit from the light-hearted approach to life that he brings. And equally, the mature Jester secretly esteems the Sage for his deep understanding and insight, and also respects his recognition that certain things in life do need to be taken seriously.

But what is it that actually causes this mutual attraction, and joins these opposites into a kind of 'special relationship'? Is it just because they see in the other something that they find hard to access in themselves?

As I wrangled with this question, I was reminded of that old saying, *'Birds of a feather flock together'*, which indicates to me that people feel comfort, security and a sense of belonging when they are with *like-minded* people.

Along the same lines, another saying states that, *'People like people who are like them'*.

So your connection with others is surely based upon what you both have *in common*, not upon your differences. And yet we also find that opposites seem to attract.

So it becomes clear that we are dealing with a paradox; as both dynamics appear to be very real.

Likeness, or familiarity, seems to meet our need for certainty; polarity seems to meets our need for variety. Both these needs are very real and what we find ourselves seeking at any given moment will depend upon which of these needs is strongest at that time. So we can see that;

Likeness creates connection:

Polarity breeds passion.

This was very helpful to understand and yet I found myself only half satisfied because I still couldn't see what exactly it was that draws these opposite characters together. I felt rather like Shen Kuo, the ancient Chinese scientist, as he grappled with the forces of magnetism. He knew that he was studying a very real and reliable phenomenon, he realised that the force he was investigating obeyed certain laws, but he had no name for it.

Complementary archetypes exist together rather like the two ends of a bar magnet; generating two opposing forces whilst remaining attached to the same magnetic bar.

If this is all true then surely it would be helpful if we were able to give this connecting bar, this imaginary magnet, a name. What we'll discover is that each pair of complementary Archetypes does have several significant connections that can be readily identified; if, that is, we ask the right questions.

These connections begin to emerge when we uncover unconscious patterns of thinking that link these complementary archetypes. Again, the simplest way to do this is to get them talking about some big, broad subjects.

As our first example, we'll ask how each archetype views the concept of *time*.

Perceptions of Time

Imagine if we'd asked each character what's important about time, we might hear them responding in these ways:

The Sovereign

"I live with a vision of better days – something we can all work towards."

The Warrior

"There's no time like the present - Just do it!"

The Sage

"We must learn from both the failures and successes of the past."

The Mystic

"The future is not bound by the past. We're free to dream and become something better."

The Lover

"Just be. Present. Now. And connect, support and nurture."

The Jester

"You have to laugh – people make the same mistakes time and time again. You know what happened the other day…"

I wonder if you picked up on some of the clues in the language that each one was using.

> The Sovereign and Mystic tend to focus on the *Future*: They're both driven by a vision of what is to come.

> The Warrior and Lover tend to focus on the *Present*: Neither of them likes to put things off – making the most of the moment drives them into action.

> The Sage and Jester tend to focus on the *Past*: Materials for both the classroom and the comedy hour are retrieved from past events.

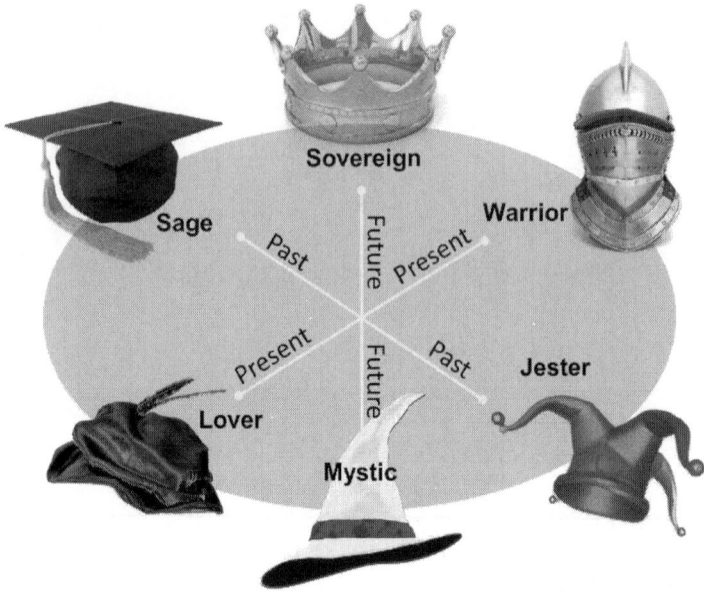

And yet 'time' is just one of many subjects we might use to uncover a common way of thinking between each of these pairs. Let's now look at the way each archetype might tackle a particular challenge that lies before them.

Modes of Operation

If we look at each of the complementary opposite archetypes in terms of their preferred methods of influence or dealing with problems, we find further threads of commonality:

The Sovereign and Mystic get things done through their *Power*.

The Warrior and Lover get things done through their *Passion*.

The Sage and Jester get things done through their *Perception*.

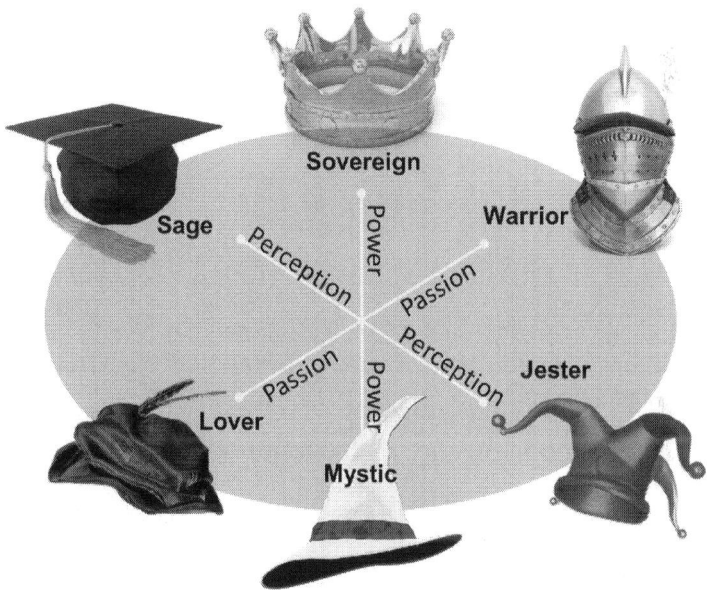

Exercise

Go back and review your personal archetypes profile. Now that you've established your dominant archetypes, you should also be able to identify the archetypes you'd expect to be drawn towards - your complementary opposites. You should expect to find a mix of traits that define your counterpart, just as there are in you.

Look at the areas that are the weakest in your profile and ask yourself if, in times past, you've been drawn to people who are strong in these areas.

Soul Mates

If there is such powerful attraction between these complementary pairs, should I now suggest that everybody should go off to find a soul mate who is their archetypal opposite?

The truth is that it's not such a good formula for a relationship that you'd want to last, because whilst passion can be ignited quickly, and answer an immediate need for variety, it can evaporate just as fast.

Long-term relationships tend to form between people of similar archetypal profiles. This is because the single most uniting factor in a relationship is the couple's shared *values*.

* * *

We've covered a lot of ground in this chapter; investigating deeper attributes of the various archetypes and exploring some vital dynamics that exist between them.

But we should ask an important question now: Are we forever to remain stuck with certain well developed archetypal traits whilst others flounder? Could these fields of ours ever produce a different kind of crop?

A general observation of life might teach us that the approach of the agriculturalist produces the most reliable results. Farmers first plough, then fertilise, then sow, then (constantly) water and wait, and eventually they harvest – each activity being carried out in due season. Thinking in this way, you might be quite suspicious of anything that promises instant results.

Yet how valuable would it be for you if I could show you how you could access the power of your archetypes in an instant? – and without any real effort at all.

CHAPTER 5 ~ Releasing Your Archetypes

"Just call out my name

And you know wherever I am

I'll come running."

Carole King

The Legend of Oakenthor

Scroll V

Armadig's old guard returned from the grove of Silvanius empty handed. They reported to the General as he watched a number of new recruits in their first weapons training exercises, a few of whom he was thinking showed promise. Armadig acknowledged the news with a silent nod and thought that Tyran must have either ditched his faith or, more likely, built another shrine to his favourite saint within his own city walls. Whatever the reason, he was nowhere to be seen that morning and Armadig was beginning to get the feeling that there would be no easy wins in this unfolding saga.

On top of that, the Absalonians had not been quick to reply to the king's offer of talks, and when they did reply two full days later, they requested the meeting another three days hence. This was clearly a delaying tactic but it was not one they could easily counter.

Sapler had not been merely pacing the castle floors in anticipation, however. True to his word, he had spent the first full day shadowing Freya – dressed as a hooded monk and going by the name of 'Brother Iago' to hide his identity – and had then accompanied Armadig all the following day as he met with captains and troops, and the scouts who had been monitoring Absalonian activities and planning the logistics around the upcoming negotiations.

On hearing that Tyran was delaying the start of the talks, King Sapler had first ensured that Armadig was gathering whatever intelligence he could, and then sent word to both Tekoia and Sagitus that he was to keep their company for the following two days.

The experience of these intensive days alongside his advisors was as enlightening as it was novel and the young King was often intrigued, sometimes in awe, and occasionally quite bemused by their ways. He noted their various methods, their remarkable insights and occasional blind spots as they carried out their daily duties. He had also seen that, for each of them, their greatest strength was quite often, in another situation, their greatest weakness.

Whilst others around them were not often aware of Sapler's identity or even his presence, his advisors had to take great pains to continue their tasks as normal; feeling a mix of pride and irritation at his constant observation of their work. However, when he asked them insightful questions about their methods, their underlying beliefs and assumptions without any hint of judgement, they all found themselves warming to him. There was an openness in this young man that was clearly absent in any previous generations of royalty this kingdom had known.

Over the course of these few days, the King found that something of these characters had begun to rub off on him. He had quite naturally absorbed some of their ways of thinking and he began to second guess them with increasing accuracy. When Sagitus felt ill after unwisely sampling some fish from a village stall, Sapler asked him if he'd mind lending him the use of his study and library, and left the old tutor to recover alone, rather than accompany the King as planned.

The King spent a long time just sitting in Sagitus' ornate 'seat of learning', joining his hands at his fingertips and musing over matters that had always been a puzzle to him. With no audience around, he even donned Sagitus' robe and walked around like the wise old teacher, muttering to himself exactly as he'd heard the sage doing as he thumbed the pages of his history books. This 'acting of the part' curiously caused his thoughts to flow in a certain sage-like way. He began to notice different things, connect aspects of their present situation to people and events in history and, when he left for his own chambers late into the evening, he felt as if could now much more readily catch the winds of wisdom in his own sails.

* * *

It was now the day before the talks. As the sun arose in a steady, regal procession toward its zenith, King Sapler sat with his counsel and confirmed a plan of action. As he addressed them they could see he was standing a little straighter than he used to, he was moving with a greater certainty and speaking with a little more authority.

"Freya, I'll need you to lead the delegation," he started. "Whilst they've made no direct statement of intent, I cannot be seen to talk face to face with an Earl who may have treacherous intent. Prepare your negotiating team and make it plain that we whilst we might grant them greater autonomy on certain grounds, we will never concede on the issue of sovereignty.

"Armadig, to help make our point, we also need a show of strength as we discussed earlier in the week. Station a substantial force, fully armed as if ready for battle, within sight of tent. Do nothing further however that might be seen as an act of provocation."

"Sagitus, I understand that your assessments and analyses have been handed over to Freya, so just be readily available to respond to any key issues that arise as the talks proceed. These discussions are unlikely to be over in a day."

"Tekoia, beyond the requests for prayer that have been sent to the priests in each shire, let me know what specific support you can give... else, there's nothing more I feel I need to ask of you."

As Sapler turned to face Hugo, the jester took a small step backwards and said, "Well, I might as well be excused as I evidently have no part to play in these games."

"Indeed, there is one very important request I wish to make of you," Sapler said with a slight smile, "By my simple tally I have one clear day ahead of these talks, and as I have spent time learning from each of others, I think I should spend this last day with you."

Hugo stood upright, feeling a mix of surprise and delight. "I would be honoured, your Majesty. I do have so many things to show you."

The King gave him a broad smile. "How about we start by heading behind the scenes of your world-famous theatre?"

"It's funny you should say that," Hugo started, "because the last time I entertained royalty backstage..." and the court jester led the King out of sight of the others, who exchanged amused glances and then set off to mobilise their people for the coming negotiations.

As Freya passed Tekoia she noticed the distant focus of her eyes and a slight frown across her brow. "Tekoia, is something troubling you about the King's plan?" she enquired as she tried to look into the mystic's face.

Her eyes still searching the space between heaven and earth, Tekoia answered, "The Earl has within his shire the warlock Barajus. He's simply left him alone in years past, but something dark seems to be stirring behind all this – unseen from our sight – and I'm beginning to think Tyran has called upon the old sorcerer to provide another dimension of support."

The women parted, both sensing that the events ahead may test them more than they'd previously imagined.

We all experience a range of emotional states through the course of an average day. Some common ones might include: appreciation, happiness, frustration, sadness, anger, thankfulness, detachment, bitterness, fascination, impatience, anxiety, loneliness, indifference, fear, exhaustion, and adventurousness.

All of these states essentially fall into one of two categories:

empowering

or

disempowering.

Being able to control your emotional state is possibly the single most important factor in any kind of performance improvement. Having the ability to switch out of a disempowering state into an empowering state would provide us with a huge advantage in any situation.

You might ask how we could gain mastery over our emotions in this way - when many would claim that it's actually their emotions that are really in charge. Does this require some sort of magic?

Triggers are Everywhere

First we should recognise that it is possible for your emotional state to change in an instant. There are many things in life that can trigger such a change; either for better or for worse.

The most popular movies tend to be the ones that the most effective at changing the emotional state of the audience – no one goes to a movie hoping they'll be unmoved.

If you haven't experienced it yourself, I'm sure you can easily imagine how a perfectly normal day would be instantly be turned sour on hearing news of a friend's accident or even death. Such an event would surely affect anyone and, however you were initially feeling, would instantly change your state.

Events like these would trigger a very similar and very deep response in every one of us. But we also each have a specific set of emotional triggers that are very personal and unique to us as individuals. Have you ever visited someone's home for the first time, used the soap in their bathroom and suddenly found yourself transported by some vivid remembrance of, say your childhood home, or a grandparent's cottage – just because the soap smelled the same as theirs? Such times don't just trigger a memory; they trigger an entire emotional state of being that you had at that time.

"Your hand may remember better if it were holding your sword."

Gandalf, in Lord of the Rings. JRR Tolkien.

What emotional state would be triggered in you if you suddenly remembered something significant from your past: your Head Teacher's voice, your first date, a family pet, your graduation day, or the first time you stepped onto the moon? Do you see how certain memories, pictures, faces, scenes, names, symbols, smells and sounds have become linked to a specific emotional response? As you're thinking of some of these things now, ask yourself are the emotions they bring up empowering or disempowering for you?

But let's turn this around for a moment: What if I was to ask you what state you trigger in others when you turn up. Is the affect *you* have on other people empowering or disempowering? Is it small, or huge?

In Tolkien's Two Towers novel, having freed King Théoden from the grip of Saraman's curse, Gandalf needed to reawaken kingly strength and authority within the still dazed sovereign. The old wizard thought that grasping his sword again might do the trick. (By now you should expect such uncommon knowledge to come from a Mystic.) It worked.

This simple, powerful trigger immediately brought back to Théoden a flood of thoughts and feelings and his kingly stature returned to him, making him ready to reassert his authority again over his realm.

Trigger-Happy

Let's review again how this actually happens.

Whenever you are in any intense emotional state, your brain will automatically link anything *unique* that is present at that same moment to the emotional state you're experiencing. Sometimes what gets connected this way has no significant meaning in itself, it just happened to be there at the time.

This may remind you of the legendary 'stimulus and response' experiments Pavlov and his dog.

What's useful for us is to know that what the brain does quite naturally and continually without any conscious guidance, can now be purposefully steered by us towards a much greater cause if we take control of this process.

The first thing to realise is that your mind is constantly linking the things you experience with your senses to the emotional and physiological states you experience in your body. Think about the way your body instantly makes a change when you're driving and hear a police siren go off just behind you – even if you're obeying the speed limit (which, of course, you are)!

Think about the way *that particular song* triggers an emotional response in you, vividly taking you back to a past event. What about when you recognise *that voice* down the end of the phone as being someone you really do not want to remember. Your brain, in fact your entire nervous system, has linked the cause and the effect.

This mechanism is very, very helpful, of course, as it enables us to learn important things very quickly. You know not to put your hand into the gas fire because you did that when you were a kid – and you learned something! It only takes one event of that intensity to for you to link forever the concept of **fire** and the experience of **pain**. After that one encounter, your behaviours will be altered forever - and in this case that's a very good thing.

What we need to recognise is that connections like these are actually being made all the time; both pleasurable and painful ones. And, not surprisingly, the more intense the pleasure or pain of the event, the stronger and longer lasting that link will be.

If some past event caused an immediate and intense response, that same state may then be triggered later in life by something very small indeed. When someone's voice or a flashing blue light is the trigger, we can see an obvious connection. But at other times our brains connect things that are completely unrelated to the event.

The connections our brains might make at the time may not be logical at all. So whilst we can safely assume that our conscious minds follow logical structures of thought, we must recognise that our unconscious minds don't care for logic in the slightest. And it is the unconscious mind that is creating these connections.

How it would sound to you if I was tell you that you could use Gandalf's knowledge to instantly unleash the power of any archetype you wished in any situation? If you can remember yourself powerfully exhibiting one of these archetypes at any time in your life, or even just imagine yourself doing so, there's a way to step up to that same level of performance – in an instant – any time you like.

Now that might all sound a bit magical but you really don't need to be a mystic to do this.

In fact, anyone can do this. It's something that I demonstrate to my clients and teach them to practise regularly and it makes direct use of this natural linking mechanism. The results are invariably nothing short of astounding.

In situations where ideas are needed fast, they release their Sage to come up with just the right answer. When they'd previously have been a bit of a push-over, the Warrior steps up and enforces a boundary. When there's discouragement and disappointment in their team, the Lover rises up to instil self-respect and a sense of personal value to each one. You get the picture.

So how can you instantly 'trigger' any one of these archetypes and do so at any time you wish?

Anyone who has studied Neuro Linguistic Programming (NLP) will already be familiar with what I'm about to describe to you – it's known as 'anchoring'.

The method is not at all complicated. We simply set up a trigger, or 'establish an anchor' by applying a little bit of pressure on a chosen knuckle whilst we are expressing one of the archetypes in full force. Once the link is made, you have the ability to trigger that archetype whenever you feel you need it, by simply applying pressure to that same knuckle in the same way that you did when you set it up.

Here we're utilising a natural function of the human nervous system and that is its ability to connect, or associate, two apparently unconnected occurrences.

We're going to connect a desirable emotional state with a simple physical action that we could perform at any time we wish.

Before I give you the step-by-step method, I want to tell you a real life story.

Keys to Success

One day during a week off with my children, I realised that I needed to get a spare set of car keys. I called my local car dealer and was told I could just arrive anytime the next morning and they'd sort it out in about 10 minutes. The next day I arrived, explained what I needed and waited... and waited. After about 20 minutes, my kids were getting rather bored and I was becoming very aware that the agreed hour to meet their grandparents was fast approaching. I approached the counter again and without any irritation simply stated "I'm just wondering when you're going to be able to sort out this spare key, as I do need to get my children to their grandparents."

The man at the counter immediately looked indignant and retorted, "You can't expect us to just drop everything and deal with you just because you've turned up – we have scheduled work to do."

I was rather taken aback and simply and calmly affirmed, "I did phone earlier and was told that this could be done for me when I arrived and that it would only take 10 minutes. I've now been waiting here over 20 minutes and as far as I can tell no one has started on the job."

The assistant (not that he was assisting me in any way) became even more defiant. "Who told you that? I never said I could do it." Not being a lover of confrontation, I could at this point feel myself getting into a bit of a state – my mouth was beginning to feel rather dry and my body was even beginning to shake a little bit.

I decided, however, that wasn't going to put up with this sort of behaviour and I managed to look right at him and say, "You haven't been in customer service very long have you?" (Ok, that was naughty – don't try that one at home.) I could tell he wanted to hit me at that point and was making great efforts to control himself. By this time a mechanic, the size of Arnold Schwarzenegger and clasping a large monkey wrench in his oily hands, appeared behind him and clearly wanted to join in.

"If you'll calm down a minute someone will help you!" Arnold said with an intense frown. If I had not needed those keys that day I would likely have walked away and let them know plainly that I would never be returning. It was clear I needed some help.

I had done just a little of this 'linking' or 'anchoring' at home in the weeks before, linking the emotional state of *unstoppable confidence* to the act of squeezing the second knuckle on my left hand. Remembering this, though I actually thought I hadn't been doing it enough for it to work effectively, I brought my hands together and gently squeezed the spot.

What surprised me most was the speed with which my entire body felt the change. Every hint of nervousness and conflict vanished in an instant, and a warm, calm energy flowed effortlessly through me. My breathing deepened, my chest naturally rose, I straightened my stance and spoke to them with a new clarity and calmness.

Stranger than that, it seemed that everyone else in the room suddenly became much more co-operative. Without many further words, they got straight on to the job and completed the task. I paid and we left without any further upsets.

Looking back I realised that it would have taken a huge amount of will power or mental gymnastics to achieve anything like the change in mental and emotional state that I achieved in that moment using a simple physical trigger. The practice at home had given me a resource that I could call upon any time I needed it in 'the real world'.

Incidentally, I noticed about 6 months later that particular garage had closed down. Maybe their other customers hadn't taken the time to establish their own state-changing anchors.

* * *

How to set an Anchor that will trigger any Archetype (any time you wish)

So, let's knuckle down to it, here's how to set up your instant trigger or, as the NLP crew would say, 'install an anchor'. (You might want to do this behind closed doors because you might appear a little strange to any onlooker as you go through this exercise.)

Step 1

Decide what archetype you would most want to have available in force and on demand. (You can select any desired emotional state, in truth, but to focus on an archetype will provide you with multiple resources simultaneously.)

Step 2

Recall a time on your past when you were very evidently thinking, talking and acting in the manner of that archetype. If you can't find a specific time, it's ok to simply imagine such a time – as long as you fully get into the part. Back in the 1950s, Maxwell Maltz popularised the understanding that your nervous system cannot tell the difference between events vividly imagined from those that are actually experience. Here's when you can directly benefit from such knowledge.

Step 3

Get back into that state of mind as fully as you can. Start to do, say and think the things you were doing at that time.

Step 4

Cause this emotional state to build even further by increasing your energy and expression; exaggerating your movements and gesticulations, speaking aloud what you were saying to yourself, feeling more of whatever you were feeling, and even moving and breathing as you did at that time.

If you recall pictures of what you saw at that time, make them bigger and brighter, closer and more intense in colour. If there were any distinct sounds in the memory, make them louder, clearer, sweeter. Let your mind amplify the memory this way – it invariably increases the desired emotional state.

Step 5

Now, as this state begins to seriously build up it's time to establish the 'anchor'. Let your right hand reach over and firmly squeeze the knuckle of your index finger on you left hand – placing the thumb of your right hand on the underside and your index finger on the top. Don't squeeze so it hurts, just apply a little pressure so that the experience is unmistakable. All the while keep doing whatever you need to in order to get into the role of your chosen archetype until it reaches its maximum expression.

Step 6

As the state begins to subside just a little, release the pressure and let go of your left hand completely.

Step 7

At this point you've provided your nervous system with a powerful emotional state and associated with it a unique physical trigger, or anchor.

A way to test if this has been done well is to clear your mind for a minute by focusing on something completely different. In fact you might even focus on something quite negative, as that will help you appreciate the difference this technique can make. Then, without doing anything to get yourself into a positive state of mind, simply apply a little pressure to that same knuckle again, just as you did when setting up the anchor.

If the anchor is set up correctly, you should immediately feel a significant change in the way you feel and the type of thoughts you're thinking. Your approach to the situation at hand will then, without any need for 'mantras' or 'affirmations', naturally be much more positive.

And now you're all set to trigger this state any time you feel you need it.

What you've now taught your brain is that the unique event of pressure on that particular knuckle is firmly associated with a certain set of thoughts, words, energies and feelings. At such moments there is actually a release of a certain cocktail of hormones (neuropeptides, if you want the technical term) in your body, which means that the change is actually a chemical thing. The next time your brain detects that type of pressure in that specific part of your body, guess what it's going to do? It will automatically trigger the release of all that 'chemical stuff' that you gave it the first time it felt that pressure.

Your unconscious mind has linked the two things together – it doesn't know any better. And that's a good thing.

If your attempts at anchoring in this way fail to significantly change your emotional state when required, make sure that:

> 1. Your mental and emotional state at the moment you apply the anchor:
>
>> a. Strongly reflects the archetype that you want to express
>>
>> b. Is very intense – something affecting your state of mind, your bodily movements, facial expressions, breathing, even your heart-rate.
>
> 2. The anchor you're applying is unique – something you don't do habitually and that isn't a common occurrence in life (like a handshake).

CHAPTER 5 ~ Releasing Your Archetypes | 129

3. You're triggering the state in exactly the same way that you set it up. Any variation from what you did and how you did it when setting up the anchor and your brain will not make the connection.

4. Do repeat the set-up exercise regularly. I tend to boost each of mine about once a week because it will fade over time.

Just one further note; I often find that the 'test' in Step 7, coming so soon after the intensity of my set up exercise, can sometimes feel somewhat less than impressive. Don't be overly concerned if that's the case with you too. The real test is triggering the state completely 'cold', when you really need it. Then you should feel the full effect of your regular rehearsals.

The trick now is to find events that would previously send you into any of those disempowering states of mind, and have ready a set of empowering archetypes linked (or anchored, as we're learning to say) to something you can trigger instantly – a set of knuckles makes this very easy, as you can anchor a separate archetype to any individual knuckle you choose.

CHAPTER 6 ~ The Shadow Side

"I don't want to let myself descend

to the shadow side again."

A-ha

The Legend of Oakenthor

Scroll VI

It had been an awful night; an unfolding of events that only the most cunning and malign of gods could have orchestrated.

All had started well enough. Freya's delegation had met with Tyran, Earl of Absalem and his key advisers late in the morning. Sitting across a make-shift but adequate table, in a large tent that would keep off the worst of the sun's heat, they began their discussions by seeking to clarify the position the Absalonian's had taken – for much had thus far been merely rumour and hearsay.

Armadig had stationed three platoons within sight of the tent, just the other side of the canal that divided the floodplain. They were an imposing force and vastly outnumbered the guards Tyran had brought with him. Largely consisting of infantry, they included the famed Old Guard, and about 50 cavalry who made sure their weaponry and banners were very visible to any observers within a mile of their camp.

In the distance, across the floodplain known as Mara Perez, was the city of the Absalonians which overshadowed their prosperous trading port. As Freya's delegation sat facing the man they had heard had become increasingly fierce and controlling over the past year or so, they were pleasantly surprised by his convivial, almost jovial, demeanour.

But unknown to any of Sapler's party, the Earl had been scheming and whilst negotiations dragged on into the night, and Armadig's troops began to doze, Tyran had secretly deployed a squad from the Warnja, a unit of personal bodyguards he'd formed from the very best of his troops, who used the cover of a low spreading mist to fill the canal with oil. The sun had long since turned its gaze towards another part of the world and on this night there was no moon. Tyran had planned this moment perfectly.

Oblivious to all this, it had become clear to Freya that her team of negotiators were fighting an increasing weariness and moments after she had requested they adjourn until morning, Tyran gave an unseen signal that set his team into action. The canals were ablaze in an instant, forming a wall of fire that separated the opposing sides and burning to ash the few bridges that straddled the wide ribbon of water. Freya's delegation and personal guards were surrounded, disarmed and bound, then rapidly carried off along the drovers' road to the fortified city.

The alarm had been sounded amongst Armadig's troops the moment the flames were seen but no one from the platoons could stand against the roaring blaze that confronted them. Even the Old Guard, who had rushed to seize the western bridge, had been driven back by a wall of ferocious flames that leapt towards them like vengeful ghosts.

Enveloped by a stifling and choking blackness; the dense black smoke of the burning oil, and the lack of any kind of natural light, captains desperately tried to regroup their scattered men and ready them for action. But they were stymied; there was simply no action they could take but move to a safe distance.

By the time the flames had subsided, the captive party and the small contingent of Absalonians were long gone, leaving nothing but an empty tent, a wide area of scorched turf and a number of large, empty, wooden, oil barrels.

* * *

King Sapler spent the following day locked away in his private chambers. Since the moment he'd been woken in the night and told of all that had transpired, made worse by an encounter at his door with Armadig who vented his fury and frustration, he'd been pounded by waves of anger and insecurity that fell upon his mind and coursed through his veins. Many hours later he was still wallowing in a pit of fear and unworthiness. He felt let down, betrayed, insecure and useless. Unable to sleep, he was now exhausted with anxiety.

After all the initial uncertainties surrounding his ascension to the throne, he thought he'd begun to perform remarkably well – especially considering his complete lack of grooming for the role. But his attempts to tackle the Absalem situation had not just failed to make progress; it had resulted in a crushing and humiliating defeat. Murmurs of discontent were rife not only in the villages but even in his own court. He had quickly become more concerned about the lack of support he felt from his closest confidents than he did about the break-away state.

"This is all hopeless." he gasped, "How can I be expected to do this? No one is any help to me. Armadig hates me for something *he* should have foreseen. The people don't respect me at all. I should never have been made king!"

Sapler had never been convinced that there was a God guiding his life, looking out for him or his people – but right now, at a time like this, he really wished there was one. If he was honest with himself – something he was finding rather hard to do at this moment - he'd have to say that he wished there was someone else who could make the decisions and he could go back to his carefree days of hunting and playing games.

But Sapler wasn't the only one struggling with a legion of personal demons. The shame of being outwitted by the Earl had sent the others down their own destructive paths.

Armadig had become a loose cannon with a short fuse; venting his frustrations on his captains, even on his own family. Infuriated by the limited role that this nervous, new King had determined for him, he now vented his repressed energies on anyone and everyone within range; openly casting aspersions upon the King and his other advisors and issuing his captains with entirely unreasonable, knee-jerk demands.

Sagitus had not been seen for a long time. He had provided specific guidance regarding the response the King should expect from the mutinous Absalonians, and had clearly underestimated their resourcefulness. Whilst the learned strategist justified his assessments to himself, Armadig had appeared, denouncing him as 'plain stupid; a mere court dummy'. Objectionable as this was, he couldn't deny he had completely missed the significance of the New Moon that week. All conversation had simply become too uncomfortable for Sagitus, so he withdrew from everyone and chose to speak to no one. Retreating to his library he distracted himself with philosophies and theories that had no bearing on the current dilemma, declaring to his battered ego that he understood things none of the others could ever aspire to.

And then, on the opposite side of the plain, Freya was also now completely alone. Confined to a solitary cell, she was trying to square with the knowledge that her belief in the goodness of others had been unfounded and her naivety had brought deeper trouble to her king. She consoled herself that it had at least been a bloodless coup, but she'd begun to wonder if anyone could actually be trusted anymore – including herself.

Overload

During a private coaching session, I had introduced my client to the whole concept of Archetypes and led him through an exercise that helped him to connect with, and release, his 'Sage' in a very powerful way. The results were immediate and, he told me later, had made a huge difference in his relationship with his fiancée. As we rounded up he asked me a very good question, "Is it possible to have *too much* of one of these archetypes?"

What we've focussed on thus far have been the healthy, mature expressions of each archetype; emphasising the good things that each one is naturally able, and inclined, to contribute. We wouldn't normally be concerned with anyone being 'too mature' or 'too healthy', but it is possible – in fact we should acknowledge that it is actually very common – for some of these archetypes to get out of balance – sometime chronically.

Something that Carl Jung recognised many years ago is that each of these archetypes also has a dark side; a characteristic set of negative behaviours that can cause real damage to both the individual and those within their circle of influence.

It is often said that someone's greatest strength is also their greatest weakness and this phenomenon can be predicted very specifically for each archetype.

This dark side will often arise with the purpose of meeting our personal needs as rapidly as possible, often when we are stressed or fearful, and it will manifest itself in two broad ways; either as *too much* of an archetype's traits, or *too little* of them.

If you can imagine each archetype being measured by its own thermometer, you can probably grasp the idea of there being a **moderate zone** of temperature that would represent the healthy, mature archetypal traits we've discussed thus far. But if the temperature rises above this zone, we'd say this character is now getting **overheated**;

and, equally, if the temperature dropped too low, the same character would become **frozen**, inactive and stifled in its expression.

H_2O

A similar metaphor we might use for this is found in the various states in which we can experience water: H_2O.

Water is, of course, vital for every kind of life. Yet it has to be at a moderate temperature for any living organism to benefit from it, because only then can we drink it or wash with it or even give it to our plants. However, if the very same water becomes too hot (or too energised, we could say) it can scald, hurt and even kill. Likewise, if it is frozen it can't be absorbed, it can't nourish us - we can't even wash things with it. Turning to ice, it can block or burst our pipes, weigh down and break our power lines, paralyse our transportation, stifle our movements, immobilise our muscles, or even kill.

So the very same substance can sustain life within a certain range of temperature and can cause much damage when too far above or below this range.

In exactly the same way, each of our archetypes can provide great benefits to us if expressed within a moderate, balanced (healthy and mature) range of temperament – and can equally do great damage outside this range; either *overheating* or *freezing*.

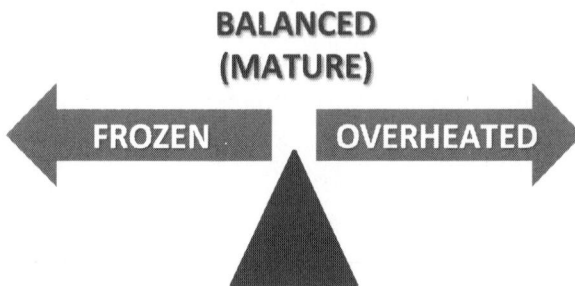

BALANCED (MATURE)

FROZEN — OVERHEATED

Summarising this:

The Balanced (or mature) zone contains all the positive qualities we've detailed so far. It should be our aim to remain in this place, where a *healthy expression* of our archetypes' key traits is evident and everyone around us benefits.

The Overheated zone is where we launch into a predictable set of *excessive expressions* that invariably cause hurt and damage to ourselves and others.

The Frozen zone represents an evident *lack of archetypal expression*. Here the individual appears unable to access the abilities and strengths of a particular archetype, even when the situation is demanding it from them, and such a lack of appropriate response will render them quite ineffective.

What's interesting is that each archetype displays very specific behaviours when it either overheats or freezes; when it operates with either too much, or too little energy.

Most people will find that their strongest traits, whilst mature and balanced much of the time, will on occasions flare up and overheat. This 'untempered' strength needs to be effectively managed if damage is to be limited.

An archetype may also dive into a 'frozen' state of inactivity – usually in response to stressful situations or a major failure after giving something their best shot. Even strong archetypes can lapse into this state when they've thrown everything they've got at a particular challenge and it is still not overcome. For under-developed or immature archetypes however it may take little more than a certain tone of voice or a certain look from someone to cause them to 'freeze up' this way.

Jung referred to these negative zones as 'shadows'; giving us a sense that the very thing that can bring us the help we need - the positive, mature archetype - also carries with it a darker side that is always present and potentially very damaging.

Too Hot to Handle

We may feel quite justified in those moments when we let our overheated behaviours fly but people around us get hurt.

Somewhere deep down inside we might have a positive intent, but we've started to exhibit unproductive behaviours, that lay too much pressure upon those around us and this invariably results in us driving people away.

If we've acted this way for years, we're probably the last ones to acknowledge that we've crossed a line and are very likely to resent anyone else pointing this out to us. Whilst we may feel completely justified in our approach at the time we're actually just over-compensating for hidden fears and insecurities.

"Roses have thorns, shining waters mud."

Sting

Kid Gloves

If you encounter someone else in an overheated state who seems intent on blaming or accusing you, there are ways to deal with it without chastising or belittling them in any way.

Of course, in the heat of the moment, it can be hard to keep calm and controlled, so a great first move is to use the anchor you've set up to trigger a specific archetype before you attempt to do or say anything in response to such a person.

You should always start by refusing to take the incident personally and let go of any need you might feel either to retaliate or do the reverse and withdraw into your shell. Triggering an appropriate archetype will sweep away the impulse to take either of these routes. Any of the six mature archetypes can actually work here, though generally either the Lover or the Sage can often work best, depending on the person involved.

Triggering the Lover, for example, you might find yourself empathising with your adversary. In this case you might express a similar passion to theirs in your voice and say something like, "That must be really annoying, especially after all you've tried to do..." and then slowly begin to decrease the heat in your own voice bit by bit as you introduce some other perspectives into the conversation. So you might say, "I wish that communications were better between us…" which would be one such way to refocus the conversation onto something you could both then seek to address. So, rather than restating the problem, you intentionally start to make a *solution* the new focus.

It's a great idea to practise this in conversations you're involved in when someone *else* is being blamed, accused or criticised in some way and see if you can change the energy of the conversation towards a more positive outcome.

I'm reminded of one particular occasion when a colleague had started to get rather overheated with me and I was starting to feel rather undermined. I heard her vent her frustrations for a bit, but when she began to get a little too personal in her comments, I simply said. "Ok, I hear you, I really do… now, do you mind if I ask you a question? Could you clarify for me your intended outcome in this conversation?"

An open question like that is sometimes a great way to steer a conversation, and I was really quite surprised how much it reduced the heat of her response on this occasion. From that place we could have a slightly more amicable discussion around the real issues.

An alternative approach is to take on the more detached position of the Sage. Your response from this position would be to calmly describe to the angry person what you're observing and how it makes you feel.

> "Harry, you are standing very close to me at the moment and you've raised your voice. When you do that, I feel (here you should state honestly how you feel inside... for example,) uncomfortable, even undermined."

Then you quite intentionally say nothing; no attempts to fill the silence with placating comments or justifications of any kind, just stay silent until after they have responded to your comment.

Such a straight-forward observation, followed by a statement about how you feel, can't really be argued with. It often disarms the assailant and their energy level is likely to drop enough for you both to find a more constructive way of discussing the issues at hand. And yes, Sages, sometimes to talk about your personal feelings is the most logical and calculated thing to do; if you research this, you should find much evidence to support this theory.

Hopefully, your assailant's next sentence will be a lot easier to manage and they can be steered towards a more constructive outcome; where you can ensure they feel acknowledged whilst making it clear that their overheated approach is not an acceptable way of behaving.

So these are two ways you can seek to deal with any overheated archetype that has confronted you head on.

But it can be equally difficult when the person you're dealing with has simply shut down.

Frozen Assets

When frozen, the archetype in question has swung into a state of complete inactivity. This shadow state of behaviour renders the mature, archetypal character, with all its innate capabilities, powerless and ineffective. The Sovereign can't make a decision, the Mystic retreats into hopelessness, the Lover becomes a loner, the Sage acts like a complete dummy, the Jester gets depressed, and the Warrior runs away at first sign of conflict.

This state of reversal often occurs when the individual believes that their present capabilities are simply not enough to deal with the situation at hand. Again, this is rarely a conscious decision; it's usually driven by an emotional state of hopelessness.

Fear, or hopelessness, can cause even a relatively well developed archetype to flip into such a negative state. Remember Maximus the Roman General after he failed to reach his family in time to save them? For weeks afterwards he practically gave up on life. The formidable warrior became a victim – even a slave - refusing to fight at all. Most people, however, wallow around in this frozen state not because of some insurmountable crisis, but because they've never invested the time or effort required to develop the specific archetype the situation demands.

Have you ever known anyone to show these tendencies in any area of their lives? I imagine you have. Maybe someone very close to you, too.

* * *

A Summary of Archetypes

So, let's combine what we've been reviewing so far and group together some descriptions that sum up each of the key archetypes; including their characteristic mature, overheated and frozen states.

As you read through each, ask yourself if you recognise anyone in your family, college or place of work who reflects any of these characteristics.

Sovereign

Balanced & Mature

Commanding, secure, decisive, just, fair and supportive, the Sovereign takes responsibility, establishes the vision, provides direction, empowers others, creates order, and sets fair and positive boundaries.   The Sovereign's primary purpose is to seek peace and prosperity of all in their realm.

Overheated: The Tyrant

Controlling, dictatorial, self-important, with a superior attitude. Must be right, perfectionist, exalts own accomplishments, refuses the counsel and advice of others. Seeks power to get their own way.

Frozen: The Slave

Avoids responsibility and decision-making, gives way to the agendas of others, blames others (especially for their own failings), lacks own vision and direction, a mere caretaker at best, paranoid, desperate for praise and respect.

Warrior

Balanced & Mature

Courageous, action-orientated, confident, competitive, enforces boundaries, finishes the job, direct, determined, disciplined, loyal and dependable. Faces and pushes through pain.

Overheated: The Savage

Hostile, compulsive, volatile, impatient, abusive, defiant, inflexible, can't stand losing. Hates to see weakness in others. Creates strife, bullying, loves to fight and cause pain. Makes mountains from mole-hills. An obsessive doer.

Frozen: The Victim

Gives way under pressure, avoids pain, avoids any kind of conflict. 'Anything for a quiet life'. Sloppy and ineffective with work. Can't finish tasks: can't say 'no'. Always procrastinating, finding reasons not to take action or even make a decision.

Sage

Balanced & Mature

Wise, learned, discerning, knowledgeable, perceptive, and hungry for truth. Rational and logical they have a healthy detachment from events, though they are often less comfortable expressing emotions. Places high value on evidence and history.

Overheated: The Hermit

Aloof, over-intellectual, entangled in impractical theory, unable to connect with real people (especially emotional ones), obsessively logical, condescending - particularly towards less educated).

Frozen: The Dummy

Immobilised through a lack of adequate knowledge or understanding (we don't know, we can't know), incapable of making decisions, pessimistic: 'everything is meaningless'.

Mystic

Balanced & Mature

Mastery of 'uncommon knowledge' and seems to draw upon unearthly powers of intuition and prescience.

Capable of bringing transformation, has faith, brings hope, and remains calm and unshaken by events. Visionary, creative and charismatic, delighting in mystery.

Overheated: The Sorcerer

Devious, condescending and superior, deceptive, secretive, manipulative, vengeful, cunning, elusive and slippery, reverts to sorcery, paranoid, Gnostic (exalting their 'higher knowledge'; declaring that 'spirit is everything').

Frozen: The Fantasist

Fearful, stressed and hopeless; lacking a belief in anything good. Easily influenced by others, doubts own abilities, lapses into continual fantasies.

Lover

Mature and Balanced

Values people, loves to build relationships and connections, empathetic, seeks harmony. Comfortable displaying emotion, playful, spontaneous, appreciates beauty - drawn to the arts, poetry and music.

Overheated: The Desperado

Lustful, desperate, infatuated, relationally restless, addictive, constantly seeking *more*.

Frozen: The Loner (or the Stoic)

Unfeeling, stoical, stuck in grief, avoids intimacy yet can't stand being alone. Numb, bored, dull. Disconnected, lacks empathy, neglects others in need.

Jester

Mature and Balanced

Brings humour, laughter, joy, colour and entertainment. Makes light of things, finds the funny side, liberates from negativity and over-seriousness.

Overheated: The Idiot

Spiteful, mean, uses humour to tear down; sarcastic and sardonic. Disruptive, easily diverted and distracted, often performing practical jokes. Flippant, can't take anything seriously, often interrupting important matters.

Frozen: The Depressive

Wallows in negativity, stuck in grief, feels shallow and insecure, lacks meaning, 'there's nothing in life to enjoy'.

* * *

I've mentioned before that every Sovereign has a Mystic close by, just as Lovers seek out Warriors and Jesters are often found colluding with Sages.

You might also have noticed that this pattern of complementary opposites can also be seen in the shadow sides of each archetype.

One of the most obvious pairs is the Tyrant and the Sorcerer. Where there's a Tyrant running the show there's usually a Sorcerer is lurking behind the scenes. (You might remember the relationship between the Sheriff of Nottingham and his witch in Kevin Costner's Robin Hood.)

CHAPTER 7 ~ The King's Quest

"It's love that holds it all together

I just had to let you know

That it's love that's holding back the weather

And the same will let it go."

King's X

The Legend of Oakenthor

Scroll VII

Tekoia opened her eyes and glanced around at the familiar surroundings of her private chambers. She had slept fitfully through most of the night until just before dawn, when she found herself caught in the afterglow of a vivid dream that had left her strangely peaceful and not a little curious.

In the dream she was walking the streets of Absalem just as the first rays of sun penetrated the valley with its pale light. She was alone, walking uphill towards the spring when she noticed other womenfolk gathering behind her, each carrying empty water vessels for their daily requirements.

On reaching the spring, Tekoia sat down to scoop up the clear, cool water to drink for herself and then proceeded to fill the vessels the town's people passed to her. But then, one by one these women started crying out, "The water is red like blood!"

Some called to their husbands, some complained to the authorities, some prayed to their gods and then, one by one, they all began to stare at Tekoia herself, with a look of terror in their faces.

This disturbed the mystic not in the slightest, however. She merely smiled, stood up and look towards the city gates below where a group of trees, which had seemingly appeared from nowhere, was now forcing its way through the city's defences.

As the dream faded, Tekoia saw all the townspeople bowing in submission before Sapler whom the trees had carried into the city square.

Noticing the time, as the emotion of the dream began to wane, Tekoia hastily noted down the key elements of the dream on a slate tablet, dressed herself and immediately headed for the King's Counsel Chamber.

Sagitus had also emerged from his libric exile earlier that morning with a new look of hope in his eye. Retreating, as he had, into his forest of manuscripts to forget all the failures of the past week, he'd stumbled across a tale in the historical accounts of the founding of Absalem on its rocky mound where a spring emerged. A curious idea had struck him and he started a search of the archives until he'd found the map of rivers he'd been looking for. Taking it in hand, though a little uncertain of the kind of reception he might receive from his sovereign, he headed straight for the King's chambers.

He was met by Armadig, who was at that moment leaving the King's presence and looking, very uncharacteristically, rather uncomfortable with himself – even sheepish. He'd evidently sought out his Commander in Chief to apologise for his recent behaviour – an act that demanded not a little humility, especially since he still regarded the King as a rather weak soul. Despite his embarrassment, he had found the King to be patient and gracious and he had left knowing the King still had confidence in his General who had promised his unswerving loyalty in the coming days.

"Don't go too far away, Armadig." Sagitus said as Armadig passed him, only briefly raising his eyes. "I'm sure there's something in what I'm about to tell the King that will require your help." With a frown and not a little uncertainty about returning to face the King so soon, the old warrior followed the sage and listened to the unfolding revelation without comment.

"I trust you have some good news for me?" asked Sapler nonchalantly as Sagitus entered the room and immediately started spreading and sorting his maps upon the table with barely a bow.

"I do believe so, your Majesty. I've found in the royal archives a map that indicates the spring in Tyran's city has its source much higher up in the Proventia mountains. Here we find several streams that disappear into sinkholes, where a thick layer of limestone meets the surface," He pointed to the map and showed where the lines marking several streams came to an abrupt end. "It's almost certain that one of these streams re-emerges as the spring in the city. The only question really is which one."

Armadig immediately the potential of this idea and launched in with his idea of a direct solution, "We should poison them all – leave nothing to chance!"

At this point Tekoia reached the chamber, bowed to the King and approached the three men and their table of charts. She wanted so much to share her dream but, as it was far from providing any specific direction, she felt she'd best hold back until she understood the current flow of discussion.

Sapler understood the opportunity before them but was adamant there had to be another way. "We'd kill more than the Absalonians if we did that, Armadig. We'd be indiscriminately killing men, women, children, livestock, sea-life; every living thing for miles downstream. I'm not ready to do that. Sagitus, how can we determine for sure which stream feeds the city's spring?"

This question visibly jolted Tekoia. "The spring ...in Absalem?" she enquired, with a look of curious wonder on her face. Then, unable to contain herself any longer, she shared a synopsis of her dream with the three men. Whilst it certainly left everyone feeling a little more optimistic, no one could draw from it a clear course of action.

Hugo, the last to appear as usual, then stepped into the room. Knowing he'd not heard any of the previous discussions, Sapler had a strange impression that the jester might still have a useful contribution to make and so asked him directly, "How would you make a stream run red, Hugo?"

Hugo thought for a moment and then announced, quite seriously, "Even if it required my own blood, I would willingly die for you, my King."

After a pregnant silence the King burst out, "By the sword of Hallmatha, that's it! Hugo..." grabbing the jester by his shoulders and looking him square in the face. "I do need you to dye for me, it would save my kingdom!" Hugo looked quite disconcerted by this remark but the King's face only beamed brighter as his plan unfolded.

"Hugo, go at once to the cloth makers and get from them as much blue, green and red dye powder as they can find and bring it all into the courtyard. Armadig, prepare three chariots and enough men to carry the sacks of dye to each of these sinkholes, and then prepare your entire fighting force ready to assault the city at sunrise.

"Sagitus, now's the time to enlist the help of the Arborians to aid us in the capture of the city. Go to them, promise we will reduce the tolls and levies that Tyran has imposed if they'll agree to unite with us and help us restore unity in the kingdom. If they are amenable, I will personally join them in the early hours and we will assault the city gates together."

As he gave his commands, everyone in this Counsel Chamber could see how the King was bringing together each of their disparate threads of knowledge and creating a plan with a clear purpose. Everyone, that is, but Hugo, who understood nothing but the fact that he would not have to sacrifice his life after all – and right now that was quite enough to be thankful for.

The Power of One

All these archetypes exist to empower, to help, to build something good. Even the warrior's strength – in its mature form – enforces good, healthy and necessary boundaries.

With wholeness being our aim, we should review how these six archetypes presently operate in our lives and uncover the issues that affect our performance and keep us from that ever-so allusive goal; our own peace of mind.

I say this because all kinds of nagging doubts, frustrations, unfulfilled desires and restless, unhappy states dissolve into the ether when we uncover and address imbalances at this archetypal level.

In all this we are seeking to make conscious some very important workings of our unconscious minds. Once we are aware of these dynamics, we can make decisions about how things ought to be. The unconscious mind is a great servant, but a pretty useless master and needs to be directed effectively if we want to put its weight behind our most important outcomes. And one of the ways we can 'talk' to our unconscious minds is to use stories and metaphors – that's what these archetypes really are.

The Essence of Leadership

It is quite possible to achieve celebrity status through the promotion of single gift or talent. But no specialist lasts very long in leadership.

Corporate leadership requires a broad range of experiential knowledge and at least a reasonable understanding of all areas of enterprise – from sales to production, HR to finance, IT to marketing. You may be a leader now, or have aspirations towards leadership. If, as you review your archetypal strengths and weaknesses, you discover that you have a real need to grow in one particular area or have a tendency to freeze or overheat in other situations then, to quote Brian Tracy, you'd do well to "courageously and repeatedly address your weakest area". Because a leader can only rise to the level of their weakest area of capability – it will forever hold him back until this is properly addressed.

Team Building

Teams work best when they combine the strengths of each individual and each one commits themselves to working towards a common aim. The team is made much more effective as the individual members each contribute their specific perspectives, skills and abilities.

Looking at their role and purpose, it's clear that specific teams will require their members to demonstrate more of certain specific archetypes than others. Team members involved in sports, firefighting or mountain rescue, for example, will all need to be strong Warriors – since *taking action* is an absolutely key part of the job for everyone on the team.

That being established, for the team to function at its best, the team captain should seek to introduce individuals with varying archetypal traits – those who will contribute their keen intelligence (the Sage), those who will ensure there was adequate nurture and support for each member (the Lover), and those who will continually encourage the team to believe in themselves and aspire to what they can truly become or achieve (the Mystic).

As a contrast I'm sure you can imagine what it would be like to work on a research team where every researcher has been chosen for their qualities as a Sage. If they completely lack any input from the Lover, they're quite likely to seek minimal contact with each other and, when they do, would spend their time talking about their own wonderful discoveries rather than how they can help and support each other to complete the tasks at hand. I may be emphasising an extreme example here, but I think you will have noticed similar patterns to this in teams that you've been a part of at some time in your life.

Maximising Motivation

Understanding the most influential archetypes in any situation is crucial if you want to motivate yourself or another member of your team.

We are all only ever drawn towards things that we value and, equally important, we are repelled away from things we detest. Understanding these forces is at the heart of motivation for any individual.

So if you need to motivate someone into action, you will have to know their personal values; what they love and what they hate. If you already have an idea of what archetypes are dominant in their lives, their primary values are quite predictable.

Have a look at the following summary and see if there's anything in here that could help you either motivate yourself, or help you to stir someone else into appropriate action.

The Sovereign

Attracted to (Above all they desire): Order, control, prosperity, power.

Repelled by: Disorder, poverty, disobedience.

Environment in which they thrive: When given responsibility to lead a group of people – or a situation where no one is leading. Respectful cooperation.

The Warrior

Attracted to (Above all they desire): Winning, results, achievement, action.

Repelled by: Losing, failure, inactivity.

Environment in which they thrive: Competitive situations. When given a clear objective or goal.

The Sage

Attracted to (Above all they desire): Specialist knowledge, learning.

Repelled by: Ignorance, emotionalism.

Environment in which they thrive: Intellectual challenges. Others asking for insight and understanding.

The Lover

Attracted to (Above all they desire): Harmony, connection, devotion.

Repelled by: Conflict, strife, insensitivity.

Environment in which they thrive: Social situations, others in need, focused one to one time.

The Mystic

Attracted to (Above all they desire): Uncommon knowledge, mystery, the power to transform.

Repelled by: Unbelief, narrow or overly logical thinking.

Environment in which they thrive: Chaos, puzzles, mystery, a need for vision/hope.

The Jester

Attracted to (Above all they desire): Laughter, fun, irony, variety.

Repelled by: Monotony, anonymity, predictability.

Environment in which they thrive: The stage. Any platform from which they can perform. Situations they can analyse to make fun of.

Without naming, and potentially embarrassing, the person I have in mind, there's a young guy I know well who is very easy to motivate because he's so competitive (a strong trait of the Warrior, as you've now begun to recognise). When there's something he simply doesn't want to do, all I need to imply is that whilst he's doing nothing, someone else is winning or benefiting and he is not – then he's up and active again.

* * *

A Double Life?

One very common issue that professional people face is that they can end up living a quite different life at work than they do at home. Now of course you'd expect there to be differences in the kind of things they have to do in these two environments but, for some people, the different roles they play have almost made them into two distinctly different people. Where this is the case, even when they are often completely unaware of this disparity, the individual invariably has a general feeling unease or unhappiness about their life as a whole.

So with wholeness being our aim, we should look at a specific technique designed to help uncover what is really going on and then bring ourselves to a place where we can be more fully who we really are – which is essential if we want to be as effective as we can be.

If you were to come to me for help in this, my initial assessment would be based upon the degree to which each of your Archetypes is active in your life – just as we did with our first profiling exercise – but this time we would create a separate profile for your personal world and your professional world. When we see them both mapped side by side, it becomes very clear where we need to start.

I remember one particular session with a corporate manager that I was coaching. I'd begun to see a little unease in him whenever certain issues were being discussed and I was pretty certain that there was something holding him back and preventing him from grasping an opportunity he had before him. I decided that I had to get to the bottom of this issue, and so I invited him to join me in a simple, yet powerful exercise that you're about to do for yourself. Looking at the results of his profile what immediately became apparent was that he was very strong in one particular archetype at work but much weaker in this same archetype at home. This difference may have been created, or at least exacerbated, by the different demands and pressures of his two main environments that had conditioned his behaviours until they became habitual patterns. Once this was made clear to him, he realised that addressing this issue would result in his greater growth and maturity...so we got to work.

I should stress that a degree of difference in archetypal expression can be very necessary between your work environment and you home environment, but if you find that you're not happy about the differences you discover, then some sort of intervention may well be in order.

So, if you had come to see me regarding almost any challenge at work, this is the specific technique I'd use to help you identify where the problem really lies:

The Technique

Step 1.

Knowing what you know about the six key archetypes: the Sovereign, the Warrior, the Sage, the Mystic, the Lover and the Jester, can you remember times and situations when each have been strongly in evidence? (This just helps you see that they are all present in some way in your life.)

Step 2.

Understand that each archetype:

- is merely a facet of yourself
- can, and does, rise or fall in influence at various times
- can be called upon at any time when their specific strengths are required
- always has a positive intent and can achieve much good, yet can become a problem if too strong or too weak in its influence

Step 3.

Using the following chart, you grade each of the six archetypes listed in terms of their influence, from 0 to 10, in your personal/home life.

	Sovereign	Warrior	Sage	Mystic	Lover	Jester
Personal Life						

Step 4.

Then do the same for your work situation – show the degree to which each of these archetypes manifest their characteristic influence in your professional life and enter a number from 0 to 10 on a row underneath.

	Sovereign	Warrior	Sage	Mystic	Lover	Jester
Personal Life						
Professional Life						

Step 5.

Look at your results and highlight the archetypes that show the greatest difference between the ratings you gave for your personal life and professional life.

This simple exercise of placing your scores side by side reveals the areas of greatest incongruence, or tension – those that almost certainly need the most work.

A difference of 1 or 2 would be quite normal, 3 or 4 indicates there may be an issue to deal with and 5 or more would indicate that things are really quite uncomfortable for you. Any number over 4 indicates that you're probably not well suited for the job you're currently doing, or alternatively, that your home environment has squeezed you into a rather uncomfortable mould.

It might be worth noting that for 99% of professional roles, you'd expect the Jester to rate relatively low and it would be no surprise to find it rated somewhat higher in your personal life - unless of course, you're a professional comedian.

Whichever way, a large difference indicates that some sort of change work is in order.

When I did this exercise with the owner of growing property company in Portugal, it became very clear to her why she was feeling completely drained at the end of each day. The work role she'd assumed was demanding far more than she was able, or ever would be able, to give. She could also immediately identify the type of person she needed to hire to handle the work she felt unsuited to deal with herself and saw the huge opportunity there was before her to play to her real strengths; focusing upon networking and client management, where she knew she would be far more effective.

So as you look at your results, ask yourself if you're completely happy with the situation that you see reflected there. If you are, then you can stop at this point and be content with a little more self-awareness.

If you're not actually happy with what the chart is revealing, and feel that you'd be a better or happier person if the differences you've highlighted could be ironed out, then you really have two possible courses of action.

The first option is to find ways to improve your performance in those weaker areas until you're comfortably matching the requirements of your role (either in your personal or professional life).

But if you decide the gap is simply too great, the second option is to change the type of job you're doing and find a role more suited to your archetypes profile.

To help you with either transition, I'd suggest you find a coach trained in the Team Me approach or at least a reputable NLP Practitioner.

One powerful technique that can help close the gap is known as a Parts Integration. It is quite hard to effectively conduct a Parts Integration on your own, but it involves asking yourself if you would like the power of the [named stronger archetype] in the one sphere of life (i.e. personal or professional) to share its influence with the [same but weaker archetype] in the other sphere.

You do need to check with the weaker 'part' if there is any reason why it would actually want to stay as it is, or if it would welcome the chance to share the strength of the stronger archetype. All being well, you would be led through a simple exercise that unites the two 'parts'; causing the separation to dissolve and releasing the stronger, more mature archetype to freely perform its role in both your personal life and your professional life.

Personal / Professional Archetype Comparison

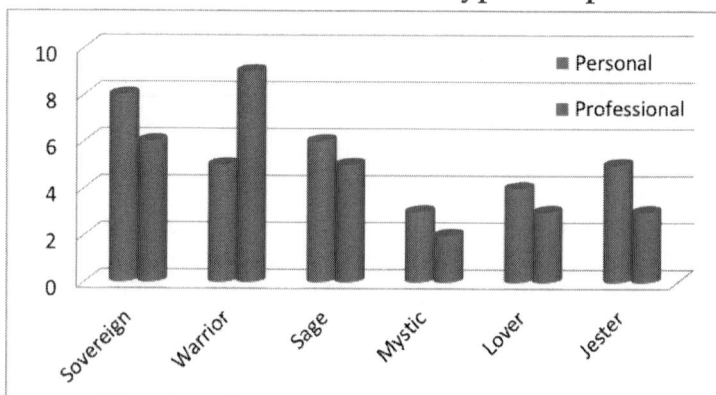

This is a real-life example of a completed chart from one of my client sessions.

With or without a Parts Integration you can, of course, always make use of your knuckle-anchored archetype to change your state and improve your performance at any given moment – triggering it in those moments when you'd normally have switched into the frame of mind of that weaker archetype.

Taking time to identify these gaps in your performance and then courageously taking continual action to meet the demands of the role at hand will bring about that *generative change* I mentioned at the start of these lessons.

This way you'll find yourself becoming so much more capable, more flexible, more confident and more effective in whatever you set your mind and hand to do.

CHAPTER 8 ~ All for One

"Just between us

I think it's time for us to realise

The differences we sometimes fear to show.

Just between us

I think it's time for us to recognise

The spaces in between

Leave room

For you and I to grow."

Rush

Bringing it all Together

Before we review everything that we've learned in this book, I would like you to stop for a moment and ask yourself a few questions. It's a good idea to write down your answers somewhere, as the very act of writing these things for yourself will help you reinforce the learning and help you to 'own' the outcome for yourself.

> 1. What has been the most helpful part of this book for you?
>
> 2. What have you already started to put into practice?
>
> 3. What appears to have given you some evident benefit?
>
> 4. Have you found yourself sharing any of these ideas with friends, family or colleagues?
>
> 5. Is there anyone else you think you should share these ideas with because of a particular situation they're in right now?

Now commit to taking action on anything you've just identified – because in the action is the learning and the growth, both for yourself and for others.

Over the course of these lessons we've covered a lot of new ground. We've learned that archetypes have been a part of our human make-up since we first appeared on Earth. Carl Jung's archetypal definitions have been around for over a hundred years, yet we (thankfully) don't need to be trained psycho-analysts to grasp the method we have before us now; a simple and highly accessible way to understand and tap into the power of these archetypes for ourselves.

We've identified six specific archetypes that form the focus of performance improvement and reviewed their unique traits in detail.

We've seen how the Sovereign, the Warrior and the Sage together display 'left-brain' thinking; being generally more rational and logical, and the Lover, the Mystic and the Jester display 'right-brain' thinking; being generally more creative, artistic and lateral in their approach to situations.

We've understood that each archetype has its own distinctive traits; both in a positive, mature and balanced form and in a darker, shadow side where things have become either overheated or frozen.

We've also looked at the way in which each archetype has its own complementary opposite and gravitates towards its counterpart to gain a bit more variety in life; the forces of passion, power and perception acting like a magnet to bring them together. When people are seeking certainty, however, they generally get alongside those who have similar archetypal traits to themselves.

All this we've understood in the knowledge that no one's character is influenced by just one archetype; we all exhibit a different mix of all six of them; with some naturally being more dominant and others being weaker.

Finally we understood that discovering the nature of these archetypes within people is possibly the easiest way to access their values, motivations, propensities and drives. It enables us to predict how they will behave in any given situation, who they would work with best and what needs they're seeking to fulfil in life, as well as understanding how they're likely to act if their needs are not met.

This is very valuable information for anyone wanting to improve their performance, who is leading a team, raising children, or simply wanting to improve a relationship.

Oh, and a little note to my Christian friends who think that all this focus on archetypes is just too New-Agey, I should remind them that their 'Sovereign' Lord also calls himself a Warrior, a Shepherd, a Father, a Lover, and Wisdom itself. The God of the Bible appears to have no problem assuming the most appropriate role of the moment and I think it would be *sage* to imitate such a model.

Conclusion

Even if you haven't actually done anything that I've been suggesting through the course of these lessons but simply taken note of the various character traits of each of these archetypes, I would hazard a guess that you will never look at people in quite the same way again. You will almost certainly begin to notice the tell-tale signs of their dominant archetypes, and their shadows, and become a little more aware of how to best handle them.

This alone puts you into a position of greater power. If you are responsible and flexible enough to manage both yourself and those you meet, on an archetypal level, you will find your effectiveness vastly improve and you potential for success will be multiplied enormously.

I look forward to meeting you one day and personally hearing your story of growth and success.

The Legend of Oakenthor

The Final Scroll

Not long before sunset, Armadig had sent three chariots laden with sacks of dye to the sinkholes that Sagitus had identified and his men had emptied the green, red and blue powder into each stream separately; not knowing where they might surface, if they would at all, or if any or all would merge at some point underground.

They had their answer as soon as the night had passed.

The wailing from within the city of Absalem was heard early the following morning by Armadig's spies who immediately passed word to the General. None of the townsfolk dared drink the water, though it was not poisoned in any way, for they had interpreted the blood-red colour as a sign that their treason against Sapler had displeased the gods and they rallied against the overlord they'd previously not dared to challenge.

When Tyran saw that he could not persuade the least of them otherwise, and received word that Armadig's men were now marching in full force towards the city, he fled for the port with only a handful of the Warnja, where he boarded his own ship and commanded they make haste for a distant, friendly harbour.

The frenzy in the streets only increased as people turned on their own guards and then set out to destroy every flag, banner and emblem of an independent Absalem that Tyran had commissioned.

The panicked sorcerer Barajus, who was trying to escape the crowd up the stairs of the Raven Tower, lost his footing, tumbled over a low balustrade and fell headlong onto a donkey track far below that encompassed the ancient city wall.

What sent the frenzied crowd into a complete panic, however, was the appearance of the Arborians approaching the city gates. Armed with longbows and spears, the sight of their surprising numbers, not to mention their heavy, shielded battering ram, was enough to cause most of the riotous crowd to scatter for safety and lock themselves indoors. Meanwhile Armadig's men had breached a section of wall near the Earl's palace and were now advancing through the streets to take up key positions throughout the city.

With few left to oppose them, it did not take long for the Arborians to breach the gate and fill the square in formation. The city's elders came and prostrated themselves before the approaching King Sapler who had joined the Arborian assault just as he had promised.

"Now we are ashamed of our ways and ask your forgiveness," they called to the King. "Tyran deceived us and promised us a mountain of lies. We submit ourselves, our city and our lands fully to you; we are your people – flesh of your flesh, bone of your bone."

King Sapler stood before the conquered city with an authority that reminded all present of King Oakenthor himself – only Sapler had some unmistakable quality about him that made every person feel that this new King was also one of their own. Amidst the dust and smoke that still swirled in the air around them, they could sense that the authority within this man was mingled with kindness; a desire to nurture as well as to command the people of this reunited kingdom. Standing in full view of them all he addressed the crowd.

"People of Absalem, you were given much and, whether out of fear or greed, you used what was given against the kingdom that had borne you. Yet, if I now have your unerring pledge as you have declared it, even this can be forgiven.

"You will not go entirely unpunished, yet if you will truly serve both King and kingdom you may keep your place amongst the provinces. Only I will expect you to aid me in the capture of the renegade Tyran and also to seek the prosperity of all the shires, not just your own welfare. I will see to it that the one who serves the most will be the greatest in this kingdom – that opportunity is now before you."

And so the kingdom was restored to order and united again that day under its rightful king. The royal standard was once more unfurled from the castle's Eagle Tower and, as he stood on the western battlement, King Sapler called to himself the members of his counsel, including Freya who had been found and released from her imprisonment.

"We have all fought with dragons without and within. Combining our strengths and working together, we have overcome whatever has opposed us. My counsel, I'm proud to have you – each of one you – at my side for your contribution has been invaluable. As we face the days to come, I will continue to call upon you, for we still have many great works to accomplish."

It was now barely afternoon. The last of the fires were being extinguished and the work of removing the debris of war had already started in the streets below. Rumours of a feast had begun to circulate and townsfolk had responded by bringing food gifts of every kind to the Great Hall.

As the King looked out across the emerald sea he appeared to be focusing his gaze on the horizon with a new intent.

"Now," he said to his counsel with a slight smile, "about those Outer Isles..."

About the Author

Pad is a Trusted Advisor to leaders in business, artists and performers across the globe. He is an international success coach and speaker and the author of *Team Me*; a dynamic approach to personal and professional performance improvement centred on an understanding of Archetypes.

He has been coaching people of all ages and from every walk of life for over 25 years; from young offenders to business owners and C-suite executives of FTSE 100 companies. Through personal coaching, live workshops and a range of ground-breaking products, Pad provides people with a powerful array of tools and techniques that enable them to take huge steps forward in their professional and personal lives.

He is Director at Come Alive Success Coaching ltd. in the UK, and Resident Success Coach at Premier Radio. He has appeared on ITV, BBC World Service, and Radio5 Live as well as quoted in The Guardian, The Independent and The Telegraph.

An NLP Trainer and Master Practitioner, he has conducted numerous training workshops and coaching sessions from the UK and Europe to the Far East.

"My mission is to get you out of 'stuck'

and to help release you into the destiny

you were created for."

Further Resources

I trust you've taken action on the exercises and recommendations woven into the pages of this book. But there's much more available to you. Simply search for 'Team Me Pad' on Google, YouTube, or Amazon to find further resources, videos, courses and an array of powerful products that can help you get clarity, then envision and empower you to new levels of success and achievement in life.

Website: **www.teamme.com**

- Sign-up now for a free Introduction Pack with Audio and PDF downloads
- Life-changing products: books, audios and online courses
- Discover the remarkable workshops, webinars and courses at **www.teamme.com/events**

Amazon: UK. http://ow.ly/HJWIA

USA. http://ow.ly/HJWC8

Audio Edition: http://ow.ly/HJWuW

YouTube: www.youtube.com/teammenow

Facebook: www.facebook.com/teammenow

Twitter: www.twitter.com/teamme

Google+: plus.google.com/+TeammePad

At a Crossroads?

How to Resolve Your Midlife Crisis and Discover a Life of True Fulfilment

by Pad

If you're at a crossroads in life, whether it's a full-blown mid-life crisis or simply a desire to find a clear and fulfilling direction in the days ahead, this is for you.

www.comealive.co.uk

Sign-up now for this unique, free video course that will guide you through powerful lessons, recommendations and insights that will help you get clear on the fundamental issues you need to address and reveals exactly how to find the path to a truly fulfilling life.

Kindle edition also available:

http://www.amazon.com/dp/B00NQ1EO9S

Cover and inside page images

Sovereign: © electriceye/Fotolia.com. Warrior: © malcam/ Fotolia.com. Sage: © Volodymyr Kyrylyuk/Fotolia.com. Lover © Andrey Kiselev. Mystic © Yan Vugenfirer / Stocklib.com. Jester: © Scott Maxwell/Fotolia.com.

Printed in Great Britain
by Amazon.co.uk, Ltd.,
Marston Gate.